# THE DEVIL'S ADVOCATE

# THE
# DEVIL'S
# ADVOCATE

*Dore Schary*

[A DRAMATIZATION OF THE NOVEL
BY MORRIS L. WEST]

*William Morrow and Company*
*New York    1961*

# THE DEVIL'S ADVOCATE
## A Play in Three Acts

PLACE: *With the exception of the first scene, which is the study of Eugenio Cardinal Marotta in Rome, the action of the play takes place in the homes of the Bishop of Valenta, Dr. Aldo Meyer, The Contessa de Sanctis and Nina Sanduzzi, in and around the village of Gemello Minore in Calabria, Italy.*

TIME: *The present; with glimpses of the past.*

# Cast of Characters
*As they appear*

MONSIGNOR BLAISE MEREDITH

EUGENE CARDINAL MAROTTA

NINA SANDUZZI

DR. ALDO MEYER

NICHOLAS BLACK

AURELIO, BISHOP OF VALENTA

THE CONTESSA, ANNE LOUISE DE SANCTIS

FATHER ANSELMO

PAOLO SANDUZZI

GIACOMO NERONE

IL LUPO

VILLAGERS, PARTISANS and SERVANTS

NOTE TO THE DESIGNER AND DIRECTOR: *The play demands a variety of sets which must present suitable playing areas. These sets should be suggested by fragments of scenery and a minimal number of props. The furniture should be sparse. Behind the swiftly changing scenes there should be a cyclorama that conveys to the watcher the age-old Calabrian mountains studded with rock outcroppings and stunted trunks of trees. The light patterns help shift the watcher's eye from place to place and also help move his mind from the present to the past. The costuming is simple and the color of the fabrics muted.*

# ACT 1

# Scene I

AT RISE: *We are in the study of* EUGENIO CARDINAL MAROTTA. *The* CARDINAL *is a short, round man, well-barbered and deceptively at ease, covering up an appetite for hard work combined with limitless energy.* HE *is bald, his domed head covered with the scarlet skullcap.* HE *is standing to the left of the desk. Opposite him, on the other side of a heavy buhl desk, to the right of his chair, is* MONSIGNOR BLAISE MEREDITH, *a gaunt figure of a man.* HE *wears a black soutane with scarlet piping. A shaft of light from a high window illuminates the cloistered and rich atmosphere of the study. The sound of the six o'clock Angelus sweeps into the room.* BOTH MEN *murmur the Latin responses and when the Angelus is concluded,* THEY *resume their conversation. As the curtain is rising we hear the conclusion of the Angelus.*

MAROTTA. Et verbum caro factum est.

MEREDITH. Et habitavit in nobis.

MAROTTA AND MEREDITH. Ave Maria, gratia plena, Dominus tecum; benedicta tu in mulieribus et benedictus fructus ventris tui, Jesus. Sancta Maria, Mater Dei, ora pro nobis peccatoribus, nunc et in hora mortis nostrae. Amen.

MAROTTA. Ora pro nobis, sancta Mater Dei.

MEREDITH. Ut digni faciamur Christi promissorum. Amen.
[THEY *cross themselves and then* MAROTTA *gestures to* MEREDITH *to sit*]

MEREDITH.
[*Sitting*]
I have been trained to prepare other men for death, Eminence. It shocks me to find I'm so unready for my own.

MAROTTA.
[*Crossing to him,* HE *puts his hand on* MEREDITH'*s shoulder*]
I grieve for you, my friend. It comes to all of us, of course, but so few of us are ever prepared.

MEREDITH. Yet we, of all people, should be.

MAROTTA. No. We are men like all the others. We are priests by choice . . . celibates by—legislation.
[HE *moves to his desk.*]
The powers we exercise and the grace we dispense—are independent of our own worthiness. It is, of course, better for us to be saints than sinners—but like our brothers outside we are generally something in between.
[*Crossing to his chair*]
It is a pious legend that the priesthood sanctifies a man. Often it's harder for us to save our souls than it is for others.

MEREDITH. I am quite empty, Eminence. There is no evil that I repent and no good that I count. I have had nothing to fight; I cannot show even scars.
[MEREDITH *makes a move to rise but* MAROTTA *indicates with a movement of his hand for* MEREDITH *to remain seated*]

MAROTTA.
[*Moving to the window*]
I can provide you with a pension. You could live quietly—

MEREDITH. Eminence—thank you for your kindness. But I have no talent for contemplation. I should prefer to go on working.

MAROTTA. One day—you will have to stop.

MEREDITH. Then I shall go into hospital.

MAROTTA.
> [*Now* MAROTTA *moves toward* MEREDITH]

Is your condition operable?

MEREDITH. Yes—but if they were to have operated—I'd have had three months.

MAROTTA. And without the operation?

MEREDITH. I shall live a while longer—but die more painfully.

MAROTTA. A grim choice.

MEREDITH. But one I have made. That is why I came back to Rome after the diagnosis.
> [*Spreading his hands in a gesture of defeat and rising from his chair as if expecting the conference is at an end*]

If it is not too much to ask I should like to be buried in Your Eminence's Church.

MAROTTA.
> [HE *nods, then returns to the desk*]

Monsignore, since you have determined to continue your work, there is a matter in which you can help me greatly—and perhaps—perhaps help yourself, too.

MEREDITH.
> [*Wryly*]

A rare opportunity, Eminence.

MAROTTA.

*[Seated in his chair by now]*

Two days ago I received a petition from the Bishop of Valenta . . . in Calabria.

MEREDITH. I have never been in Calabria.

MAROTTA. It is a run-down diocese. But the Bishop has helped keep the majority for the Christian Democrats—an accomplishment which earned him a Pontifical letter of commendation.

MEREDITH. Well deserved?

MAROTTA. The support came from the Monarchists—not from converted Communists.

MEREDITH. But apparently he has a flair for politics.

MAROTTA. Indeed.

*[Looking at papers]*

The petition forwarded was for the introduction of the Cause for Beatification of a Servant of God—Giacomo Nerone. He asks me to appoint a Devil's Advocate. It is simple, my friend, to find a Postulator to build the case and present it.

*[A pause]*

But it is difficult to find a Devil's Advocate—a Promoter of the Faith to destroy the case.

MEREDITH. It usually is.

*[Again a pause as* MAROTTA *consults his papers and rises from his chair]*

MAROTTA. Giacomo Nerone was a man murdered in 1945 by Communist partisans under circumstances which are claimed, may well be called martyrdom. Since his death, he has received veneration from many villages, and several cures of a miraculous nature are attributed to his influence. The Bishop of Valenta is a canny man. If the investigation goes well—he has a rod to beat the Communists. If it goes badly—the Church in Rome bears most of the blame.

MEREDITH.
  [*Becoming interested*]
It's a political move and I mistrust it.

MAROTTA. Man is a political animal who has an immortal soul.

MEREDITH. But too many saints can bring sanctity into disrepute. I have always believed that our function at the Congregation of Rites—was not to put saints into the Calendar —but to keep them out.

MAROTTA. True. But the motion has been sent to us. We have no authority to forbid the investigation.

MEREDITH. We might advise against it.

MAROTTA. On what grounds?

MEREDITH. Discretion. We are on the eve of elections. Giacomo—

MAROTTA.
  [*Sitting at desk*]
—Nerone.

MEREDITH.
  [*As* HE *moves close to* MAROTTA]
—Nerone was murdered by Communists in the last year of the war. What do we want to do? Use him, to win a provincial seat—or as an example of heroic charity?

MAROTTA. I imagine our brother Bishop would like to have it both ways. But the first investigation has been made and the verdict leans toward approval. The next step is automatic. The introduction of the Cause for Beatification to the Bishop of Valenta's own court.

MEREDITH. And once that happens, it takes on the look of a carnival. Newspaper accounts—local merchants hawking relics. It can't be avoided.

MAROTTA. We may be able to control it.
   [*Rising*]
For precisely all the reasons you have mentioned I would like you to become the Devil's Advocate.

MEREDITH.
   [*With surprise and some apprehension*]
I am a dying man, Eminence. I could not do you justice.

MAROTTA. Let me judge that. Besides, as I said, it may help you too.

MEREDITH.
   [*Shaking his head*]
How?

MAROTTA.
   [*Moving again from his desk to* MEREDITH]
What I have to say, Monsignore, is probably a presumption. I believe you have reached a crisis. You are like many of us here in Rome, a professional priest—no stigma in that. There are many who fall short of that limited perfection— a good professional. Yet—now—now—you have perhaps discovered it is not enough.
   [HE *pauses*]

Perhaps like many you have lost touch with the people who keep us in touch with God.

[MEREDITH *eyes* MAROTTA *and sees the truth in what has been said*]

That is why this investigation may help you. It takes you from Rome—to one of the most depressed areas in Italy. You will live with simple people as you try to rebuild the life of a dead man from the evidence of those who lived with him—the poor—the ignorant—the dispossessed.

[HE *places a sympathetic hand on* MEREDITH's *shoulder*]

Among them perhaps you will find the cure for your own sickness of spirit.

MEREDITH.

[*Wearily*]

What is my sickness, Eminence?

MAROTTA. There is no passion in your life, my son. You have never loved a woman, nor hated a man, nor pitied a child. You have asked nothing and given nothing. This is why you have doubts and fears—because a man who cannot love his fellows cannot love God either.

MEREDITH.

[*Sitting*]

I am so very tired.

MAROTTA. Go home and rest.

[*Abruptly and quite businesslike*]

In the morning you can leave for Calabria. Present your credentials to the Bishop of Valenta and begin work.

[MEREDITH *watches, then pulls air into his lungs deeply*]

MEREDITH.

[*Rising*]

You are a hard man, Eminence.

MAROTTA.
[*His voice firm*]
Men die every day.
[*Then softly*]
Some are damned, some achieve salvation. But the work of
the Church continues.
[HE *holds out his hand.* MEREDITH, *with proper obeisance, kisses
the ring*]
Go, my son—in peace and in the name of God.
[*The* LIGHTS DIM *and the scene shifts as* MEREDITH *exits the
study*]

# Scene II

*The* LIGHTS COME UP *in* DR. ALDO MEYER's *home in Gemello
Minore. It is the home of a poor man. It appears to be a place
where a man lives for a short period of time before moving on.
It lacks personal effects. It is clean and tidy.*

*The main room which we see is used for a waiting room and
also serves as* DR. MEYER's *living and dining room. To one side
is an office and examining room. The backstage wall is a com-
bination kitchen and storeroom.*

AT RISE: *It is late afternoon.* TWO WOMEN, *with their heads
hooded by black shawls, sit on the sofa in the room fingering
rosary beads, their prayers unintelligible to us. One of them
is* SIGNORA MARTINO. *The* OTHER *is her oldest daughter.* NINA
SANDUZZI, *a strong, swarthy woman who is thirty-six years old,
comes from the office and crosses to them.* SIGNORA MART NO
*rises.*

NINA. Your prayers have been heard. The Dottore says Martino will live.

SIGNORA MARTINO. Let him say it to me.

NINA. I say it. It is the truth.

SIGNORA MARTINO. Let the Dottore say it to me. When I look into his face I will know if it is true.

NINA.
[*To the* DAUGHTER *as* SHE *rises*]
Take your mother and go to your home.
[NINA *moves toward the hutch*]

SIGNORA MARTINO. She cannot carry me and I will not go.
[*The* DAUGHTER *pulls on her* MOTHER's *sleeve. The* MOTHER *angrily slaps her* DAUGHTER's *face*]
First I will see the Jew-man.
[DR. ALDO MEYER *now appears from the examining room. His shirt sleeves are rolled up and* HE *carries his bag to the couch toward the* WOMEN]

MEYER.
[*Looking at* SIGNORA MARTINO *steadily*]
Your man will live.
[SHE *stares into his face*]
You believe me?

SIGNORA MARTINO.
[*After a pause*]
I believe.

MEYER.
[*Moving to bookcase—putting instruments down*]
He's as strong as an ox. Go to your home—feed your children. Later we will get your husband home.

SIGNORA MARTINO. Why did he fall into his forge? He was not drinking?

MEYER. No, he was not drunk. He suffered a slight stroke. . . . His burns are more serious. But he's strong as an ox and he will live.

SIGNORA MARTINO. To work the anvil? Or will he be like Rossi's man—unable to move?

MEYER. It is too early to say.
[*All through this exchange* SIGNORA MARTINO *has stared at* MEYER. *Now satisfied,* SHE *turns to go, beckoning her* DAUGHTER *to follow*]

NINA.
[*After the* WOMEN *have gone*]
She believed your lie?

MEYER.
[HE *crosses to the screen, puts on his jacket and sits at the table as* NINA *serves him*]
It was no lie. He'll live but he will never be able to work.

NINA. There are six children.

MEYER. Too many.

NINA.
[*Putting food on* MEYER's *plate*]
Who is to feed them?

MEYER. They won't starve. Public relief.

NINA. Bah! A dozen interviews and hundreds of printed forms—for a kilo of pasta. What answer is that?
[SHE *replaces the pan on the stove*]

MEYER. The only one I know today. I used to have others
—but no one would listen. They liked the old way. Well—
this is the old way.

NINA. You know what Giacomo would have done?
  [MEYER *nods mockingly*]

NINA.
  [*Continuing*]
He'd have gone to Martino's forge and worked it himself.
He'd have knocked on every door and begged for help for
Martino. He'd have gone up the hill to the Contessa's villa
and pleaded for money and for work for Martino's wife—
he'd have—

MEYER.
  [*Cutting in harshly*]
Yes—he was a remarkable man, your Giacomo.
  [NINA *crosses to hutch and pours water*]
That's why they killed him. And Martino—
  [HE *gestures toward the examining room*]
was one of the firing squad.
  [*At that moment* NICHOLAS BLACK *enters.* HE *wears a bright red
  shirt, faded denims, rope sandals and a battered straw hat.* HE
  *is in his middle thirties*]

BLACK.
  [*With a sweep of his hat*]
I bring you greetings, Dottore.
  [NINA *takes a glass of water and without a word goes into the
  examining room.* BLACK *watches her go*]
Why, Doctor, you surprise me. I've never seen her before.
  [HE *slaps his rump*]
She has the look.

MEYER. She has a house of her own. She comes each day to clean and cook for me.

BLACK. I'd like to paint her.

MEYER. I wouldn't advise it.

BLACK. Why not?

MEYER. She is the mother of the boy who has been posing for you, Paolo Sanduzzi.

[BLACK *half-turns away and then after a look back at the* DOCTOR *crosses to a cheese platter on the hutch and cuts himself a chunk*]

BLACK. I was in Valenta yesterday to pick up paints and canvases—the place is humming. The news has also reached Gemello Maggiore.

MEYER. What news?

BLACK. This saint of yours, Nerone. They're going to beatify him.

MEYER.
    [*Not impressed*]
They've been talking about it for a year.

BLACK.
    [*Sitting*]
Ah, but now they've stopped talking and now it is in process. Notices are posted on the churches—and the people are being called to give evidence. And at the Bishop's home is a visitor from Rome—a Devil's Advocate. He'll be coming here in a few days.

MEYER. Are you sure of that?

BLACK. Certain of it. The visitor, a Monsignore, is English and will be the Contessa's guest when he arrives at Minore. This place will be famous.

MEYER. That's what I'm afraid of.

BLACK. Why? You're not even a Catholic. It's no concern of yours.

MEYER. You don't understand.

BLACK. What if I don't understand all of it?
    [MEYER *looks off in the direction of the examining room*]
I'm dying to see what happens when they start digging up the real truth about Giacomo Nerone. I intended to leave next week—but now I think I'll stay.

MEYER.
    [*Suddenly angry*]
Why did you come here in the first place?

BLACK.
    [*With a flutter of his hand*]
Simple. I had an exhibition in Rome. The Contessa bought three of my canvases and with the check invited me here to paint for a while—
    [*Then sarcastically*]
She is in the tradition of great patrons. Are your reasons for being here so simple?

MEYER. No—no. I've been here for nineteen years—I'm Italian and yet sometimes I feel as alien as you must feel. More so. I am a Jew. Exiled here during the war.

BLACK. Reason enough for being unhappy.

MEYER. But I know my reasons for unhappiness. Do you know yours?

BLACK.
[*Pointing to his chest*]
You've never met a more happy man.

MEYER.
[*Shaking his head*]
No. I think you are very unhappy. . . . You are looking for something you will never find. Go away, Nicholas Black. Leave the Contessa. Leave Paolo Sanduzzi. You truly don't belong here. You speak our language but you don't understand us.

BLACK. I do indeed. You've all been hiding something for years—and now it's going to be dug up.
[MEYER *turns away*]
You knew Nerone?

MEYER.
[*Casually*]
I knew him.

BLACK. Was he a saint?

MEYER. I know nothing about saints. I only know men.

BLACK. And Nerone?

MEYER. Was a man.

BLACK. What about the miracles?

MEYER. I've never seen a miracle.

BLACK. Do you believe in them?

MEYER. No.

BLACK. Then why, my dear Doctor, are you afraid of this investigation?

MEYER. It is late. I have a patient in my office.

BLACK.
[*Preparing to leave*]
I'd almost forgotten. The Contessa would like you to dine with her tomorrow night. She asked me to plead with you to accept.

MEYER. No need to plead. My thanks to the Contessa.
[NINA *enters*]
I'll be happy to come.

BLACK. Ci vedremo. And good evening, Mrs. Sanduzzi.
[HE *exits as* NINA *crosses and prepares to leave the house*]

MEYER. How is Martino?

NINA. His pulse is good. His breathing is easier.

MEYER.
[*Sitting at the table*]
Then he can be moved tonight.

NINA. I will call some of the men. They will take him.
[MEYER *nods*]
What news did the painter bring?

MEYER. A priest has arrived in Valenta to sit as Devil's Advocate in the Bishop's court. He will come to Minore in a few days.

NINA. He will ask questions, like the others?

MEYER. More than the others.

NINA. Then the answers will be the same—nothing.

MEYER. No, Nina, not this time. Now Rome is interested. The press will be interested. Better they get the truth.

NINA. You say that?

MEYER.
  [*Pointing*]
Who can drown the shouting in Maggiore? It is what they want to build a new church. Even Rome has heard the sound. Let's tell them what they want. Maybe then they will leave us in peace.

NINA. Why do they want it?
  [*Now* SHE *is angry*]
What difference does it make? They called him all sorts of things when he lived—now they want to call him a "beato." It's just another name. It doesn't change what he was—a good man, my man.

MEYER.
  [*Rising and going to her*]
They don't want a man, Nina. They want a saint with a gold plate on his head. The people want it because they can get on their knees and beg for favors instead of working— or fighting for favors.

NINA. Then why should I help them?

MEYER. Because if we tell the truth, they'll drop the case. Giacomo was a good man—but he was no more a saint than —Martino.

NINA. Is that what you believe?

MEYER. Don't you, Nina?
  [SHE *doesn't answer*]

Don't you?
[HE *is below table*]

NINA.

[*In a whisper*]
I know he was a saint. I know he did miracles, because I saw them.

MEYER.

[*Losing his temper*]
God Almighty, Nina. Even you? . . . He slept in your bed. He gave you Paolo, a bastard child, but never married you. And you tell me he was a saint. Then if you believe that, why didn't you tell the priests? Why don't you join the people in Maggiore who want him as a new saint?

NINA. Because he would never have wanted it. Because it was the one thing he asked—that I should never tell what I knew about him.

MEYER. What then will you say, Nina, when they point to your boy, Paolo, and say, "There is a saint's son and he makes himself a femmenella for the English painter"?
[NINA *stares at him for a long moment, then speaks quietly*]

NINA. What do I say when they point to me in the street and whisper, "There is the one who was a saint's whore"? What?
[MEYER *doesn't answer*]
Nothing—
[MEYER *moves back to the table*]
Nothing at all!
[SHE *crosses to him*]
Do you know why, Dottore? Because he made me a promise before he died.

[SHE *stands motionless, remembering each word*]
"No matter what happens, cara, I shall look after you and the boy. They can kill me, but they cannot stop me caring for you." I believed him then. I believe him now. Paolo is foolish, but he is not lost.

MEYER. He will be, damn soon. Go—call the men.
[NINA *takes her bag and starts out of the house*]
Nina—I'm to be at the Contessa's house for dinner tomorrow night.
[NINA *has turned to look at him*]
When I am there I will tell her about Martino and ask her to help.

NINA.
[*Steps toward him*]
Dottore—there is a saying—after the loud thunder comes the soft rain.

MEYER. I also have a saying—when a man is hungry—let him eat.
[NINA *exits.* MEYER *looks at his food and slowly begins to eat. The* LIGHTS DIM OUT]


# Scene III

*The* LIGHTS COME UP SLOWLY *in the dining patio of the villa of* AURELIO, BISHOP OF VALENTA. *Sunlight illumines the corner of the patio, half-enclosed, half-open to the soft air. In the background can be seen the landscape of the Calabrian hills.*

AT RISE: A SERVANT, *gnarled with years, is pouring the coffee.* HE *crosses to the buffet.*

*Standing in the archway looking out is the* BISHOP. HE *is a tall, lean man in his middle fifties.* HE *has iron-gray hair and fine, aquiline features.* HE *turns toward the* SERVANT. MEREDITH *enters.*

AURELIO. Thank you, Mario.

SERVANT.
   [*With a nod*]
Excellenza.

AURELIO. The Monsignor and I will be occupied for a while.

SERVANT. Yes, Excellenza.
   [HE *exits as the* BISHOP *nods*]

AURELIO.
   [*Turning toward* MEREDITH]
Are you certain you don't need a doctor?

MEREDITH. Certain, your Lordship. These spasms I get are old and familiar enemies.

AURELIO. The Calabrians say that the country air has healing powers.

MEREDITH. It's a welcome change from Rome. And unexpected. . . . I know this is a tired land, eroded and dry. And yet here you have acres of oranges and olives—and beauty.

AURELIO. It's an experiment.
   [MEREDITH *questions him with a glance*]
An experiment in practical education. I was born in the north. My people were mountain farmers—good ones.
   [THEY *both move toward the table*]
These people in the South imagine the clergy are born in

cassocks and that their only talent is for swinging censers in the Cathedral.

[MEREDITH *sits*]

I bought this place from a landowner who was up to his eyes in debt and I am farming it with half-a-dozen lads to whom I try to teach methods of modern agriculture.

MEREDITH. How goes the experiment?

AURELIO. It is a battle—but I think I am winning.

[HE *sits*]

I have also made the villa my official residence. The old one was hopelessly antiquated. I have handed it over to my Vicar General. He loves it—he is one of the old school. You are surprised, Monsignore?

MEREDITH. Pleasantly.

AURELIO. Did you expect velvet and brocade and gilt cherubs with the paint peeling off their backsides?

MEREDITH. Something like that.

AURELIO. You will find enough of the past here in the South. Feudalism, reaction—old men following old ways and totally unprepared for the new. They see poverty and ignorance as burdens to be carried—not as injustices to be remedied.

MEREDITH. And what do they think of the Church?

AURELIO. They believe in more priests, more monks, more nuns. I'd like to see fewer and better ones. I'd prefer fewer churches and more people going to them.

MEREDITH. Fewer saints, too?

[AURELIO *looks at him sharply, then suddenly laughs*]

AURELIO. Thank God for the English!
[*Rises and crosses to the sideboard and brings a platter of cheese to the table*]
A little skepticism is good for all of us. You wonder why a man like me should take up the cause of Giacomo Nerone?

MEREDITH. Frankly, yes.

AURELIO. Until you came, my dear Meredith, I was beginning to feel I had made a mistake.
[HE *looks back at* MEREDITH]
I mean by appealing to Rome for assistance.

MEREDITH. Why, your Lordship?

AURELIO. Modernizers are always suspect . . .
[HE *sits*]
especially here. If they succeed—their conservative colleagues are irritated by the implied reproach.
[MEREDITH *cuts cheese and eats*]
If they fail—it is charged they tried to do too much, too fast —and the old ways endure. So I've found it wiser to go my own way and keep my affairs to myself—and leave the critics to make the first move.

MEREDITH. Who are your critics, Lordship?

AURELIO. The landowners—and they have strong voices in Rome. Some of the clergy find me too indifferent to local ritual and tradition. The politicos distrust me, because I preach that the party is less important than the individual who represents it.

MEREDITH. Do you find support in Rome?

AURELIO. You know Rome better than I do, my friend. If I succeed, well and good. If I fail—they'll nod their heads wisely and say they've been expecting it for years. So I prefer to keep them guessing. The less they know—the freer I am.

MEREDITH.

[*Rises from the table, crosses to coffee and fills his cup again*]
Then why did you write to Cardinal Marotta? Why did you ask for Roman priests as Postulator and Promoter of the Faith?

AURELIO.

[*Slowly, not looking at* MEREDITH]
Because this is new ground to me. I understand goodness but I'm unfamiliar with sanctity. I believe in miracles—but I never expected to find them performed on my own doorstep.
[HE *now looks up*]
That's why I applied to the Congregation of Rites.
[HE *smiles*]
You are experts in these matters.

MEREDITH.

[*Turning to face* AURELIO]
Was this the only reason?

AURELIO. You talk like an inquisitor.

MEREDITH.

[*Returning to the table*]
I am, your Lordship. I am the Devil's Advocate.

AURELIO.

[*With a nod*]
What other reason could there be?

MEREDITH. Politics. Election politics.
[AURELIO *slaps the table with the palm of one hand*]

AURELIO.

[*Smiling*]

So that's it. I wondered why his Eminence was so co-opera-tive. I wondered why he's sent an Englishman instead of an Italian.

[*Now the smile leaves his face*]

But Marotta is wrong. Quite wrong. That's what can hap-pen in Rome. Clever fellows like Marotta get too clever for everyone else's good.

[HE *crosses near* MEREDITH]

I've two reasons for being interested in this case.

[HE *holds up a finger*]

One—the veneration for Nerone has become an unauthor-ized cultus. I have to investigate it—for approval or con-demnation.

[*Another finger joins the first*]

Two—

[HE *hesitates*]

—it isn't so simple—and the officials wouldn't understand it.

MEREDITH. Marotta might. I might too.

AURELIO. Very well—I'll try to explain. I believe that the Church in this country is in drastic need of reform. I think we have too many saints and not enough sanctity—too many medals and not enough medicine—too many churches and not enough schools. We have millions of men out of work and millions of women living by prostitution. A tree is known by its fruits, and I believe that it's better to pro-claim a new deal in social justice than a new attribute to the Blessed Virgin.

[HE *pauses*]

Do I shock you, Monsignore?

MEREDITH. You encourage me. But why do you want a new saint?

AURELIO. I don't. I'm committed to pressing the case, but I hope, with all my heart, that it fails. I hope that you, as the Devil's Advocate, destroy the case.

AURELIO. The mayor of Gemello Maggiore has collected fifteen million lire to advance the cause—and will not give me a thousand for an orphanage. If Giacomo Nerone is beatified, they will want a new church to house him. I want nursing nuns—an agricultural advisor and twenty-thousand fruit trees from California.

MEREDITH.
   [*Rising*]
But, your Lordship, suppose the case is proved? Suppose Nerone really is a saint and a wonder-worker?

AURELIO. I'll wait on the facts. When would you like to begin work?

MEREDITH. Immediately. I'd like to spend a few days studying the documents. Then I'll move into the twin villages to begin taking depositions.

AURELIO. There is some advice I would like to offer.

MEREDITH. I welcome it.

AURELIO. It is my opinion that you will not find the truth about Giacomo Nerone in Gemello Maggiore—the larger twin—because it is there he is buried and there where they make profit from his memory. In Gemello Minore—the little twin—it's quite another story. There in Gemello Minore he was murdered—and there you will find the truth provided you get them to tell it to you.

MEREDITH. Whom should I see first?

AURELIO. I have written to Contessa de Sanctis and asked her to put you up in her villa. Through her you will meet the others. You are tired—and in pain. Have a good rest. I will see you at dinner.

MEREDITH. I am grateful, your Lordship, more grateful than I can say. I am a sick man—and lonely. You have made me feel at home.

AURELIO. We are brothers in a big family. I'm glad to be of service. I hope you will regard this house as your house and myself as your friend.

MEREDITH. Thank you.

[MEREDITH *exits toward his bedroom as the* LIGHTS DIM OUT]


# Scene IV

*A patio adjoining the villa of* CONTESSA ANNE LOUISE DE SANCTIS, *high above the valley between Gemello Maggiore and Gemello Minore. A stone wall about five feet high lines the edge of the patio, and above it can be seen the landscape. The patio furniture is lovely and serviceable. The limbs of an olive tree shade part of the patio. What can be seen of the villa is beautiful and costly.*

AT RISE: *As the* LIGHTS COME UP *to a* LATE AFTERNOON GLOW, BLACK *is observed sitting on the edge of the wall, sketching the valley below him. In a moment the* CONTESSA *appears.* SHE *is dressed in a well-tailored dinner gown.* SHE *is impeccably groomed, daintily scented and powdered.* SHE *is in her middle forties; her body is as firm as a woman in her early thirties. But there is a weariness in her manner, a result of memories of too many men, not enough love and too much sleeping medicine.* SHE *sees* BLACK *and half-turns away from him as* SHE *speaks quietly.*

CONTESSA. Nicki, please don't sit there.

BLACK. Very well.
[*The* CONTESSA *has her back to him.* HE *smiles and then carefully moves his body to a standing position on the wall.* HE *assumes the pose of a colossus*]
Now you may look.
[*The* CONTESSA *turns, gasps and again turns away*]

CONTESSA. That doesn't amuse me, Nicki.
[BLACK *jumps to the patio*]

BLACK. I have returned to earth.

CONTESSA.
[*Now angry, as* SHE *faces* BLACK]
You know that terrifies me.

BLACK. But the view is so lovely. A three-thousand-foot bird's-eye view of the valley. I'll hold your hand while you look.

CONTESSA.
[*Sitting in chair above table*]
The thought nauseates me.
[SHE *rubs her temple*]
I'll be happy when you leave here.

BLACK. Anne, I've changed my plans.
[HE *takes his sketch pad and begins to draw a sketch of her*]

CONTESSA. How have you changed your plans?

BLACK. The Bishop of Valenta has asked you to accept Monsignor Meredith as a house guest. True?

CONTESSA. True.

BLACK. So I have decided to stay on for a few weeks to assist you and bask in the reflected glory of this honor paid to you.

CONTESSA. Frankly the honor hasn't overwhelmed me. The Monsignor is a sick man and illness frightens me.

BLACK. But he is a countryman of ours. Your dear dead husband would have greeted the Monsignor's arrival with cymbal and trumpet.

CONTESSA. My dear dead husband would have done no such thing. He hated the English. His greatest compliment to me was that I seemed more Italian than British.

BLACK. But he was a reverent Catholic.

CONTESSA. That didn't stop him from blowing out his brains in Libya when his unit was surrounded by the English.
    [BLACK *rises and shows the sketch* HE's *drawn to the* CONTESSA]

CONTESSA.
    [*With an intimate chuckle*]
Nicki—that's wicked.
    [BLACK *places the sketch book on the table*]

BLACK. Honor or no honor, my dear, it occurred to me that we will have an inside seat on the investigation.

CONTESSA. I suppose so.

BLACK. There will be all manner of interesting tidbits.
[HE *eyes her carefully*]
Come to think of it, you'll probably be a witness. You knew Nerone?

CONTESSA.
[*Uneasily*]
Only slightly.

BLACK. But at any rate, we'll have a box seat at a village comedy.
[*A pause*]
And in a few moments Dr. Meyer—one of the leading characters will be here to provide the first amusement.

CONTESSA. I can cope with Dr. Meyer. It's the Monsignor who worries me. I'm uneasy and my neck is tied in knots.

BLACK. Does the oncoming investigation of the life and times of Giacomo Nerone make you uneasy?

CONTESSA. I have no relish for it.

BLACK. You are at a great advantage. The Devil's Advocate in your villa—and innumerable opportunities to offer what you care to offer—or discredit what you choose to discredit. The great trick, cara, is to turn a risky situation into something of advantage to yourself.

CONTESSA. Monsignor Meredith will be no fool—no country priest susceptible to flattery.

BLACK. I will be here to help.

CONTESSA. Ah! Then the cause is lost.
[SHE *rubs her neck again*]
All you've done is add to my uneasiness.

BLACK. You have at hand the best masseur in all of Italy. My fingers are smooth—my touch, a caress.

CONTESSA.

[*With a smile*]

Prove it.

[BLACK *crosses behind her.* HE *places a cushion behind her neck and then slowly begins his massage of her neck and the sides of her face*]

BLACK. That's it, Anne, let go.

[HE *continues his massage*]

You have beautiful skin, cara. Supple as a girl's. Some women lose that very quickly. You're a lucky one.

[*The* CONTESSA *enjoys the massage, and the mood of the scene now becomes more intimate and sensual*]

I've often wondered why you never married again; why an attractive woman would choose to bury herself in the wild hills of Calabria. You're not poor. You could live anywhere —London, Rome, Paris—

CONTESSA. I've been there, Nicki. I like to visit Rome. But this is my home. I always come back.

BLACK. You haven't answered my question.

[*There is a pause as* HE *moves his fingers over her jaws and neck*]

You're tense again. Let go, Anne.

CONTESSA. I've been married, Nicki. I've been in love. I've had proposals and I've had affairs. None of them really satisfied me. It's as simple as that.

BLACK. It's not that simple.

[*Her head against his stomach*]

CONTESSA. You've never married, darling. Why?

[*This turns the tables on* BLACK]

BLACK.

[*Trying to pass it off*]

I've never needed marriage.

[*A pause*]

I've always managed to get what I want without it.

CONTESSA.

[*Mockingly*]

You gay bachelors.

BLACK. If there weren't gay bachelors, there wouldn't be merry widows—only frustrated ones.

CONTESSA. Do you ever get frustrated, Nicki?

BLACK.

[*His hands stopping for a moment*]

With you, cara, how could any man be frustrated?

CONTESSA. Thank you.

[*Without a wasted move, the* CONTESSA *takes* BLACK'*s right hand and slides it down her dress to her breast. Quickly* HE *withdraws his hand and moves away. The* CONTESSA *laughs*]

Poor Nicki. Didn't you think I knew?

BLACK. I don't know what you're talking about.

CONTESSA.

[*Rising*]

I'm talking about your being—different. . . . That you don't really care for women. That you're head over heels and gone for young Paolo Sanduzzi. That's true, isn't it?

[BLACK *moves away. The* CONTESSA *goes to him, no longer laughing.* SHE *touches his arm*]

No need to be angry. You don't have to have secrets from me.

[BLACK *wrenches himself away.* HE *crosses to the wall. Then*

HE *waits a moment and, regaining his composure,* HE *crosses back to the* CONTESSA *and speaks to her in a level voice*]

BLACK.

[*Turning to her*]

It's no secret, Anne. I like the boy. I think I could do a great deal for him. I'd like to get him out of that benighted village—have him educated and give him a decent start in life.

[HE *looks away from her*]

I haven't much money, God knows, but I'd be willing to put out every penny for that.

CONTESSA.

[*Turns to him—soft but ironic*]

And what would you want in return?

[*Slowly* BLACK *turns, stares at her and speaks softly*]

BLACK. Nothing. Nothing at all. But I don't expect you to believe it.

CONTESSA. I do believe you, Nicki.

[SHE *begins to massage* BLACK's *neck*]

And I think I might help you to get him.

BLACK. Why?

CONTESSA.

[*With a slight smile*]

I have my reasons. But I mean what I say. You help me with this priest and I'll help you with Paolo Sanduzzi.

[BLACK *eyes her steadily*]

Is that a bargain?

BLACK.

[*Believing her*]

It's a bargain, cara.

[HE *takes her right hand and clasps it in his hands, raises it to his lips and kisses it.* SHE *rumples his hair. At that moment* DR. ALDO MEYER *enters.* HE *is dressed in a neat but old blue suit. The* CONTESSA *immediately crosses to him as* BLACK *rises and approaches the tray of drinks and ice which is on the commode*]

MEYER. Good evening, Contessa.

CONTESSA. Dear Dottore—how nice to see you. It's been too long since your last visit.

BLACK. Doctor—can I fix you a drink?

MEYER. Thank you—wine and soda, please.
[BLACK *prepares the drinks*]

CONTESSA. I can't tell you how delighted I am that you're here.

MEYER. Is this dinner a special occasion? You see I'm dressed for a party.

CONTESSA. No—I thought it would be pleasant for us to be alone and have a chat about many things.

BLACK.
[*To* MEYER, *as* HE *serves the drinks*]
Do we have an agenda of subjects—or do we pick one at random?

MEYER. The Contessa usually finds a way of gracefully getting around to what really interests her.

BLACK.
[*Handing them the drinks*]
I had no idea that you and the Contessa had such an intimate friendship.

MEYER. I believe that the Contessa and I share mutual respect and mistrust.

CONTESSA. Precisely.

BLACK. My compliments to both of you. Doctor—do you have any opinion about the probable outcome of the elections in Italy?

MEYER None.

BLACK. Well, do you have any reservations about the Church becoming involved in political life?

MEYER. I do think that the Vatican has lost some standing through its identification with a political party.

BLACK. And yet it is strange that there is still great reverence for the Church in Italy, and so much irreverence for the priest.

MEYER.
[*With a shrug*]
The more priests you get, the more their faults show up.

CONTESSA. Speaking of priests. I wonder what Monsignor Meredith will be like?

BLACK.
[*To* MEYER]
Yes—I wonder.
[MEYER *looks from the* CONTESSA *to* BLACK. HE *gets the message that this is the real topic of the evening*]

MEYER. I don't.
[HE *eyes them both a moment*]
He comes—then goes away. That's all.
[*A pause*]

I have a problem of my own—which I wanted to discuss with you, Contessa.

CONTESSA.
[*Stymied for the moment*]
What sort of problem?

MEYER. Martino, the blacksmith, had a stroke yesterday. His family are going to need help. I wondered if you'd make some money available. And also if you'd take two of his daughters into service here, Teresina and Rosetta. They are old enough to begin work.

CONTESSA.
[*Casually—seizing the bargaining moment*]
Of course. It's the least I can do. The truth is I've been thinking quite a lot about the young people. There's nothing for them here.
[SHE *leans over toward* MEYER *and continues persuasively*]
I think it's time to revive some of your plans, Doctor—to create work for them.

MEYER.
[*Nodding*]
Good.

CONTESSA. For instance—Paolo Sanduzzi. Nicki tells me the boy is intelligent and willing. He could be brought here and set to work with the gardeners. No doubt his mother could use the money.
[MEYER *doesn't answer*]
Don't you think so?

MEYER. If you can use him, why not? You'd have to discuss it with his mother, of course.

BLACK. Why?

MEYER.
  [*To* BLACK]
Because he's under age.
  [*Then to the* CONTESSA]
His mother is still his legal guardian.

CONTESSA. Of course I'd want to speak to her. Would you ask her to see me tomorrow?

MEYER. I'll ask her. But she may not care to come.

CONTESSA. That's her affair.

MEYER. You were asking about the Monsignor. I had a letter from the Bishop today. He tells me the Monsignor is to be your house guest.

BLACK. The Contessa is concerned he'll be a nuisance. He's apparently ill.

MEYER. Quite. He's dying of cancer.

CONTESSA. How awful.

MEYER. There's a room in my place. Not too comfortable —but adequate.

CONTESSA. He'll stay here. There are servants to look after him—and you'll be able to visit him whenever necessary.

MEYER.
  [*Softly*]
I was sure you'd say that.

BLACK. I wonder what he'll be like—our Monsignor Meredith? Probably pinched and gray.

MEYER. Very likely. Cancer tends to spoil a man's complexion.

BLACK. I hope he's not crotchety. He's English, which of course should make a difference. I'm anxious to see what this Devil's Advocate makes of the love affair of Giacomo Nerone.

MEYER. What do you know about it?

BLACK. A little more each day. Yesterday I learned that his mistress does your housework. And I employ his illegitimate son as a model. But perhaps the Church will overlook all this. Perhaps the lists need a penitent—come back to God! Great opportunists, these clerics! Sin and be damned—repent and be hallowed!

MEYER. I'm a Jew. I have small taste for Catholicism—but even less for blasphemy. I'd like to change the subject.

CONTESSA. Nicki—we're going to have dinner in a few minutes—you ought to get dressed.
[BLACK *exits*]
Now, Doctor, we're alone—you're irritated—have your say—
[MEYER *shakes his head*]

MEYER. You wouldn't thank me.

CONTESSA. Try me. Tell me nicely—what's wrong with me —and what's your prescription?

MEYER. First—the prescription. Stop stuffing yourself with barbiturates. Stop collecting oddities like Nicholas Black, who tell you dirty stories and give you no joy. Sell this place. Go to Rome. Then get married to a man who'll keep you happy in bed and make you keep him happy.

CONTESSA.
> [*With a smile*]

You've got a dirty mind, Doctor.

MEYER. It gets dirtier. You've retired after a bad marriage and many affairs because you failed yourself and your men. . . . Yes—you've retired to your own private world of mental pornography that drives you crazy with desire and dissatisfaction. It's dangerous. You end up with gigolos and fellows like Black and an overdose of sedatives. You've time. You can still be a lover.

CONTESSA. How do I get a husband? Buy one?

MEYER. You'd probably do better with an honest bargain than with a dishonest love.

CONTESSA. Anything else, Doctor?

MEYER. Only one thing. Get Nerone off your mind. Stop trying to strike at him through Nina and the boy.

CONTESSA. I only want to do something for Nerone's son. Give Paolo a good start in life.

MEYER. What would you do with him, Contessa? Hand him to your painter?

CONTESSA.
> [*Turning to him*]

Why, Doctor, you do have a dirty mind.
> [SHE *takes his arm and leads him toward the dining room. The* LIGHTS DIM OUT]

# Scene V

*The* LIGHTS COME UP *in the* BISHOP OF VALENTA'S *villa.*

AT RISE: BLAISE MEREDITH *is seated near the open arch above the table. The table before him is covered with books and bound records. The lights are on and it is evening.* MEREDITH *has been reading but now* HE *stops and rubs his eyes with weariness.* AURELIO *enters.*

AURELIO.
  [*At sideboard*]
Still at it, my friend?

MEREDITH. I'm stuck.

AURELIO.
  [HE *takes an apple and moves toward the table*]
These things take time. What do you find so difficult?
  [HE *sits*]

MEREDITH. There's an indefinable—I'm searching for evidence of sanctity—heroic virtue. So far I've found none. I have no clear picture of Nerone nor of the witnesses themselves.

AURELIO. They explain some of my own doubts about this matter. No elements of conflict or controversy in any of the depositions. And saints are, generally, unusually controversial people.

MEREDITH. There are also elements of secrecy.

AURELIO. Precisely.

MEREDITH. Most of the testimonies to date come from the residents of Gemello Maggiore.

AURELIO.
   [*Slicing the apple*]
They have most to gain. They want that new church—the prosperity that will come from the pilgrims—all the rest of it.

MEREDITH. And no one in Gemello Minore has testified. Not even the local priest, Father Anselmo.

AURELIO. Father Anselmo is not a sturdy pillar of the Church. He is sometimes spiteful—and most times too fond of the grape.

MEREDITH. Why not clear him out?

AURELIO. He's also old. He's been a priest for a long time. I don't want to drive him deeper into despair. But he's not the only reluctant one in Minore—there are the others—all of them—well—perhaps they all have most to hide.

MEREDITH. Perhaps—but I've found no answer to the obvious question, why? Why do the people who seem to have known him best refuse to speak of him—Nina Sanduzzi—Dr. Meyer—

AURELIO. He is to be your doctor in Gemello Minore. I've also written him about you.

MEREDITH. Thank you. But why does Meyer refuse to give any testimony?

AURELIO. I don't know. I do know that before and again after the war Meyer himself had tried to organize these people for their benefit—but he failed completely. He's a man of extraordinary humanity but handicapped by being a Jew in a Catholic country—perhaps by other things.

[HE *rises*]

You will be talking to him. But you see, as yet, no saint in Nerone?

MEREDITH. Not yet. He has compassion, and a talent and taste for leadership. And he is grateful. Godliness, perhaps, but not sanctity. But the mystery—without the reported miracles—is heavy. Who is Nerone? Where does he come from? Why do the people he has helped execute him? Why? Nerone hadn't forgotten them. He was still with them.

AURELIO. Perhaps all we have is a story of a good man caught up in politics.

MEREDITH.

[*Also on his feet by now*]

Does your Lordship really believe that?

AURELIO. Does it matter what I believe, Monsignore?

[*The* TWO MEN *look at each other for a long moment.* AURELIO *has a faint smile on his lips*]

MEREDITH. Does it matter? I think it matters much.

AURELIO. Why, Monsignore?

MEREDITH. Because, your Lordship, I think that you, like me, are afraid of the finger of God.

[AURELIO *walks close to* MEREDITH, *then slowly turns away.* MEREDITH *stands rigid, staring at* AURELIO's *back. After a moment* AURELIO *turns to him*]

AURELIO. You are right, Meredith. I am afraid of the finger of God. I am. I sit on a high pinnacle. I am subject only to the Pontiff. I am lonely and often puzzled. As I am by this matter of Giacomo Nerone.

[HE *moves close to* MEREDITH]

I told you I do not want a saint. But what if God wants him?

MEREDITH. Then we shall find a sign.

AURELIO. In the miracles of Nerone?

[MEREDITH *doesn't answer*]

You are dissatisfied with the miracles of Nerone?

MEREDITH. I'm the Devil's Advocate. It is my business to be dissatisfied.

[HE *indicates the papers on the table*]

Of all the depositions I've read, only three show some conformity to the Canonical demands . . .

[HE *sits at the table*]

a cure of an elderly woman suffering multiple sclerosis; the mayor of Gemello Maggiore, who claims he was cured of a spinal injury; and a child dying of meningitis who recovered after an application of a relic of Giacomo Nerone. But these—will require a rigid examination before we go halfway to accepting them.

AURELIO. I wonder what happened in the old days when medical knowledge was limited and the rules of evidence were less stringent? Isn't it possible that many miracles then accepted weren't miracles at all?

[HE *sits*]

MEREDITH. Very probably. Do you believe in saints, your Lordship?

AURELIO. I do. I believe in miracles as I believe in God, who can suspend the laws of His own making. I believe, too, that the hand of God writes simply and plainly, for all men to read. I am doubtful of His presence in confusion and conflicting voices.

MEREDITH.

[*Rising*]

As I am doubtful of the miracles of Giacomo Nerone?

[HE *walks to the sideboard and picks up an orange and holds it*]

There are miracles all around us. The miracle of an orange tree—the miracle of design that spins our universe. But still people want a sign—a new sign.

[HE *crosses to the records and taps them*]

And if they don't get it from God they turn to palmists and astrologers and table-tappers. What do these depositions mean but that people demand wonders in the sky and miracles on earth?

AURELIO.

[*His voice flat*]

Sometimes they get them.

[MEREDITH *looks sharply at* AURELIO. AURELIO *rises and crosses to* MEREDITH *above chair and places a hand on* MEREDITH'S *shoulder*]

I ask you again, Meredith. What if God wants a new saint whose name is Nerone? You, too, are puzzled and afraid of the finger of God. I find then, in you, a brother whom I have come to love and to trust. We are both looking for a sign.

[*Suddenly* MEREDITH *winces as a shaft of pain hits his body.* AURELIO *crosses for a glass of water as* MEREDITH *reaches into his soutane for his pills.* HE *swallows them with some of the water* AURELIO *brings to him.* AURELIO *holds* MEREDITH's *shoulder as the spasm eases*]

I have prayed for both of us.

MEREDITH.

[*Tonelessly*]

Sometimes at night I feel the life slipping out of me. When the pain is hard—I cry out—but with no prayer—only in fear. I kneel and recite the Rosary but the words are empty. I feel so alone—I am grateful that your Lordship prays for me.

AURELIO. Yes—I have prayed.

[MEREDITH *looks up at him*]

And out of prayer, I have come to a decision. We should ask for a sign.

MEREDITH. What sign?

AURELIO.

[*Slowly*]

This is the prayer we should make—both of us. "If it is Your will, oh God, to show the virtue of your servant Giacomo Nerone, show it in the body of Blaise Meredith. Restore him to health and hold him longer from the hands of death through Jesus Christ, our Lord."

MEREDITH. No! No!

AURELIO. If not for yourself—for me!

MEREDITH.

[*Rising*]

No! No!

AURELIO.

[*Ruthlessly*]

Why not? Do you deny omnipotence?

MEREDITH. I believe in it.

AURELIO. And mercy?

MEREDITH. That, too.

AURELIO. But not for yourself?

MEREDITH.
   [*Rapidly*]
I do not deserve it.

AURELIO. Mercy is given, not earned.

MEREDITH. I will not ask for it. I cannot. I dare not.

AURELIO.
   [*The fast tempo of the scene stops*]
You will ask for it.
   [*Then gently*]
Not for yourself. Because I, your friend, ask you.
   [*There is a long pause*]

MEREDITH.
   [*Softly*]
But if the words fail—I am in greater darkness—not know-
ing whether I have presumed too much or believed too little.
   [HE *halts for a breath*]
Your Lordship lays a new cross on my back.

AURELIO.
   [*Reassuringly*]
It is a strong back, Meredith. Stronger than you know.
And you may yet carry Christ on it across the river.

                                        *End of Act I*

# ACT 2

# Scene I

*At the* CURTAIN *the* LIGHTS ARE UP *in the* CONTESSA'*s patio. It is morning just before twelve o'clock.*

A T   R I S E : BLACK, *dressed in slacks, blue blazer and a sports shirt, lounges against the wall and then moves toward the coffee table as the maid brings in a tray holding a wine bottle and glasses.* BLACK *helps himself to a glass of wine as the* MAID *exits and the* CONTESSA *enters.* SHE *is dressed in a beautiful linen dress. As* SHE *enters,* SHE *is angry and until* MEREDITH *enters,* BLACK *and* SHE *talk in quiet albeit tense voices.*

BLACK. Does the Monsignor approve of his quarters?

CONTESSA. You were damned rude to him.

BLACK. I hardly said a word.

CONTESSA. That's what made you rude.

BLACK. Cara, what did you expect me to do? Kiss his back-side and ask him to bless my medals?

CONTESSA. For God's sake, Nicki, shut up!

BLACK. I hardly had any opportunity to say anything even if I had wanted to. You took over the reception in elegant style. Not too little—not too much—the charming chatelaine welcoming the Church—the expatriate English lady doing honor to a fellow-countryman. Very impressive. You must be ready for conversion.

CONTESSA. Nicki—you're a nice enough little man and a middling good painter. You have your problems and I've promised to help. I've my problems—and don't complicate them by being clever.

BLACK. I'll be the soul of understanding.

CONTESSA. If you're not prepared to behave, you can pack your bags and I'll have you driven to Valenta in time to catch the next train to Rome.
[BLACK *knows* SHE *means it*]

BLACK. I'm penitent. I'll behave. I promise.
[HE *takes her hand*]
Please forgive me, cara.
[HE *kisses her hand*]

CONTESSA.
[*Suddenly patting his cheek and smiling*]
Be a good boy.
[MEREDITH *enters from the house.* BLACK *adjusts his hair and greets* MEREDITH *with a generous smile*]

MEREDITH. Contessa, your home is a delight.
[BLACK *takes a glass of wine and brings it to* MEREDITH, *who has moved closer to the wall to get a view*]

BLACK. The view, Monsignore, is extraordinary. The valley is a thing of beauty from this distance.

CONTESSA.
[*Lifting her glass*]
To your success, Monsignore.
[MEREDITH *nods and* BLACK *and the* CONTESSA *sip their drinks*]

MEREDITH. And to you and your health, Contessa.
[HE *sips*]

CONTESSA. You must forgive my ignorance, Monsignore. But I have been wondering—how do you get started working on a case like this?

MEREDITH. There are actually no rules. First you read the depositions, then you talk to as many people as possible—then you compare and collate the information. Later, when the Bishop's court is set up, there are more questions and cross-examinations under oath—and in secrecy.

CONTESSA. But where do you start—? I mean—with this one.

MEREDITH.
[*With a smile*]
Your knowledge of local conditions could be a very good preparation for me. I had hoped you might be able to help me first.
[BLACK *looks over at the* CONTESSA, *but the* CONTESSA *parries* MEREDITH *with calm*]

CONTESSA. I'm happy to do anything I can. But being English, I live a different life and think differently from these people. I could be quite wrong in my ideas. I thought I could be most helpful by having you meet Dr. Meyer and the parish priest. They know so much more about the village.
[SHE *rises*]
Don't you agree, Nicki?

BLACK. Of course. I'm sure you're right.
[HE *moves closer to* MEREDITH]
You see, Monsignore, this is a strange country. You have to be part of it to understand it.

MEREDITH.

[*Blandly*]

You're the experts. I appreciate the trouble you're taking for me.

CONTESSA. Please excuse me. I'll see about lunch—and greet our other guests.

[MEREDITH *nods as the* CONTESSA *exits.* BLACK *eyes* MEREDITH *appraisingly*]

BLACK. I hope you will let me paint you, Monsignore. You have an interesting face and expressive hands.

MEREDITH. This village must have better subjects than I, Mr. Black.

BLACK.

[*With a grin*]

You provide the contrast. The courtly Roman among the provincials. I wonder what you'll make of the gallery of characters you'll meet here.

MEREDITH.

[*Aware* HE'*s being goaded*]

I'm wondering, too.

BLACK.

[*Mockingly*]

Frankly, I don't really understand how one could possibly consider beatifying a man who seduces a village girl, gives her a bastard son and then leaves her.

MEREDITH.

[*Admitting the humor*]

It presents problems. But it doesn't necessarily put the case out of court. In strict theology, one cannot ignore the possibility of sudden and miraculous conversion.

BLACK. *If* one believes in miracles.

MEREDITH. If one believes in God, one believes in miracles.

BLACK. I don't believe in God.

MEREDITH. It's a tough world without Him. It's rough enough with Him.

BLACK.
[*Pressing the argument*]
I'd like to believe. But there's so much professional Mumbo-Jumbo. And so many mysteries.

MEREDITH. If there were no mysteries, there would be no need for faith.

BLACK. You'll need faith unraveling the mysteries here concerning Nerone. Why won't people speak of him—not even the Contessa?

MEREDITH.
[*With interest*]
Did she know him then?

BLACK.
[*Guilelessly*]
Oh, I thought you were aware of that.
[*The* CONTESSA, *followed by* FATHER ANSELMO, *enters. As* MEREDITH *turns to them,* BLACK *smiles to himself in satisfaction at having planted the first spear.* ANSELMO, *a priest of sixty, is ill-kempt and arthritic*]

CONTESSA. Monsignor Meredith, Father Anselmo—
[ANSELMO *takes a glass of wine from the table as he crosses to* MEREDITH. *The* TWO CLERICS *greet each other*]

ANSELMO. Glad to meet you, Monsignore. We don't get many Romans down this way. Too far and too rough for 'em, I suppose.

MEREDITH.
[*Not wanting to debate it*]
I suppose.

ANSELMO. That's our trouble here—the Vatican doesn't even know what's going on. I remember when—

MEREDITH. His Lordship sends you his kindest greetings and hopes that I won't be too much trouble to you.

ANSELMO. His Lordship sends his greetings! Nice of him. I'm a flea in his ear—and he'd like to get rid of me. Monsignore—we might as well understand each other.
[DR. MEYER *now appears on the patio*]

MEREDITH.
[*To* ANSELMO]
I don't see why we shouldn't get along.

CONTESSA.
[*As* MEYER *enters*]
Monsignore—Dr. Meyer.

MEREDITH.
[*Delighted to leave* ANSELMO]
I'm happy to meet my medical adviser. I'm going to be in good hands.

MEYER. Reserve your judgment, Monsignore. I have a bad reputation.

MEREDITH. I'll take that chance.

MEYER. Perhaps—tomorrow—I'd like to examine you.

MEREDITH. I'll be there in the morning.

CONTESSA.
[*Placing a chair for* MEREDITH]
Monsignore.
[*To* MEYER]
About young Paolo, Doctor—is he coming to work for me?

MEYER. I believe so. His mother will probably come to see you soon.

CONTESSA. I'm glad.
[SHE *turns to* MEREDITH]
This is of interest to you, Monsignore. Young Paolo San-duzzi is, of course, the son of Giacomo Nerone. He was baptized with his mother's name.

ANSELMO. Ha!

CONTESSA. He's rather wild—but we—the Doctor and I—thought work would be good for him. I've offered him a job as assistant gardener.

MEREDITH. That seems kind. How does his mother live?

MEYER. She works for me.

MEREDITH. Oh.
[*By now the* ENTIRE GROUP *is seated around the coffee table*]

ANSELMO. Used to be pretty. She's thickened up now. I remember when she made her first Communion. Lovely child.

MEREDITH.
[*To* MEYER]
You knew Nerone—

ANSELMO.
*[To himself]*
Lovely child.

MEREDITH. You knew Nerone, Doctor?

MEYER. Yes. I was the first person who saw him after Nina Sanduzzi.

MEREDITH. You're probably aware, Doctor, that in a cause for beatification even the evidence of non-Catholics is admitted if they are willing to give it.

MEYER.
*[With a smile]*
I know. Though we are denied entrance into your Heaven, we are allowed to aid the safe passage of others.

MEREDITH. Would you, at your convenience, talk to me about Nerone?

MEYER. Tomorrow, we can exchange examinations.

CONTESSA.
*[To MEREDITH]*
Father Anselmo can probably help you a good deal. He's very close to all our people.

ANSELMO.
*[Wiping some wine off his chin]*
I never thought much of Nerone. He interfered too much. Used to come battering on my door as soon as anyone had a bellyache. Wanted me to go racing out with the Sacraments. One night he almost had me shot by the Germans. After that, I'd lock up after curfew.

MEREDITH. Having the Germans must have made it uncomfortable for everyone.

CONTESSA. Indeed. They took over this villa. I was under open arrest most of the time. It was dreadful. I was always afraid.

MEREDITH.
  [*To the* CONTESSA]
First evidence seems to indicate that Nerone acted as a kind of mediator between the peasants and the Germans.

CONTESSA. An exaggeration, Monsignore.

BLACK. Has anyone ever established definitely who this man was and where he came from?

MEREDITH. It seems not. Only that he was a deserter. He claimed his home was Reggio but there are no records that such a man ever lived there.

BLACK. Interesting. If he were a deserter, he couldn't be a saint, could he?

MEYER. Why not?

BLACK. I'm no theologian, of course; but every soldier takes an oath of service. To break such an oath would be a sin, wouldn't it, Monsignore?

MEREDITH. It would.

BLACK. And a deserter would be living in a constant state of sin.

MEREDITH. For a non-believer, Mr. Black, you have a very Christian logic.

BLACK. It seems like obvious logic.

MEREDITH. There may be other facts. For instance, a man cannot bind himself by oath to commit sin. If a sin is required of him under an oath of service—he is obliged to refuse it.

ANSELMO.
[*Now impatient with wine and memories*]
Trouble is, Monsignore—you've become Roman. You don't see the simplest things—even when they stick up under your nose.
[*There is a pause and an uneasiness. The* SERVANT *enters and approaches the* CONTESSA]
Everybody's talking as though they knew nothing. We all knew who he was.
[*The* CONTESSA *rises*]
I knew. The Doctor knew. The—

CONTESSA. Father Anselmo! Lunch is served. Monsignore—
[SHE *takes* MEREDITH'*s arm and leads him into the villa*]

ANSELMO.
[*Following the* CONTESSA]
Everybody knows—nobody wants to say anything—I knew who he was—the Dottore knew—
[THEY *exit.* MEYER *watches them go, then rises and looks at* BLACK *before he exits*]

BLACK. Should be a lively lunch!

MEYER. Go to hell.
[*The* LIGHTS DIM OUT SLOWLY *as the scene ends*]

# Scene II

*The* LIGHTS GO UP *in* MEYER'S *home.* NINA *is in the room with her son,* PAOLO, *a lean, handsome boy of fifteen.* NINA *is slicking down his hair.* DR. MEYER *is concluding a conversation with one of his patients—an extraordinarily pregnant* WOMAN.

MEYER. It will be a few days—then all will be well.

WOMAN. It never goes well with me.

MEYER. I will be there to help you this time.

WOMAN.
> [*As* SHE *exits*]

I will also pray to Saint Anne.

MEYER. Fine—but when you feel pain, call me.
> [*After* SHE *exits*]

Last time she prayed—and at the last moment was afraid of the Jew doctor—and lost the baby. Well, Nina, what will she do this time?

NINA. I'm not here for riddles, Doctor.
> [SHE *indicates her son*]

You want to speak to Paolo.
> [PAOLO *is apprehensive and shy as* MEYER *extends his hand to him. After a moment,* HE *exchanges a brief handclasp*]

MEYER. You are growing into a good-looking man, Paolo —almost sixteen.
> [*There is a pause.* MEYER *looks at* NINA]

Perhaps you could fix things up in my office?

[HE *sits on the couch.* NINA *nods and then retreats into the office*]

Sit down, Paolo.

[*As* NINA *exits,* PAOLO *looks at her.* SHE *gestures to him to sit.* PAOLO *sits on the sofa, tugging at his tight shirt collar*]

Open it, Paolo.

[*Gratefully* PAOLO *does just that. There is a pause*]

Yes, you are growing into a good-looking man.

[PAOLO *nods*]

Your mother has spoken to you about working for the Contessa?

[PAOLO *nods*]

You know young Rosetta Martino is going to the villa?

[PAOLO *nods. This provokes* MEYER *into some temper and* HE *rises*]

Paolo, a conversation has to be between two people. Now you are one—we are two. So let's talk.

[PAOLO *nods*]

Well, how do you feel about you and Rosetta working at the villa?

[*There is a pause*]

Do you want to go—or not?

PAOLO. I'll go.

MEYER. With your pay—you can help your mother—and still have something for yourself.

PAOLO. Yes.

MEYER. The beginning of a man's life is most important. Usually a father tries to help his son to the right direction. You haven't a father—so—I'd like to help instead.

PAOLO. But I don't need any help.

MEYER. We all need help. You need it because of the English painter who likes you and puzzles you.

[PAOLO *turns away*]

You know about men and women, Paolo?

[PAOLO *looks at him and there is a faint smile*]

PAOLO. I know about Rosetta.

MEYER. And so you know how they come to kiss and caress and what happens when they make love. But does it puzzle you that you feel what you do about Rosetta—and yet feel something of the same when the Englishman touches you?

PAOLO. He has never touched me.

MEYER. Good. Then there's nothing to shame you.

PAOLO. I am old enough to think he would like to.

MEYER. Remember, Paolo—when a man's body and heart wake up from their early sleep—they can be bent one way or the other—like the wind that bends the sapling. And after a while the sapling bent with the wind grows into a tree with its own shape. The proper way for a man to grow is toward a woman.

PAOLO. Then why am I going to work at the villa? The painter is there.

MEYER. He will not be there long. And Rosetta will be there to remind you which way to—to grow.

PAOLO.

[*Suddenly rising and shouting*]

He tells me he will take me to Rome. He will get me out of Gemello.

[NINA *enters*]

I can go with him where people don't know about me or my father or my mother. Where they will not call me a saint's bastard—

[MEYER *moves threateningly toward him*]

MEYER. Paolo!

NINA. No—Dottore!

[*Slowly*]

Paolo—I loved your father and he loved me.

PAOLO. Then why didn't he marry you?

NINA. He had his reasons.

PAOLO. You say I am a man. Then talk to me as a man. ·

NINA. I will, Paolo. But first tell me what you call me, in your heart.

[NINA *looks at him.* PAOLO *brushes at his eyes as if to clear the hair from his face—then slowly* HE *turns away from* NINA]

MEYER. Your mother asked you a question.

NINA.

[*With a gesture to* MEYER]

He'll answer me.

[PAOLO *is motionless and silent.* MEYER *makes a move toward him and* NINA *again halts him*]

He'll answer—maybe not now—but sometime.

[NINA *moves toward* PAOLO *and puts a hand on his shoulder. There is a knock on the door.* MEYER *looks at them both, then crosses to the door, opens it, and* MEREDITH *enters*]

MEYER. Monsignore— Come in—come in.

MEREDITH. Good morning, Dottore.

[MEYER *makes a gesture of welcome.* HE *looks at* MEREDITH, *his doctor's eye instantly telling him that* MEREDITH *is in pain though* MEREDITH *makes every effort to fight against the bitter agony of his body.* PAOLO *rises.* NINA *gets her bag.* THEY *both face* MEREDITH]

MEYER. This is Nina Sanduzzi and her son, Paolo.
[MEREDITH *nods.* NINA *and* PAOLO *make the proper obsequies*]

MEREDITH. I have wanted to meet you both.

NINA. Yes, I know.

MEREDITH. I would like to talk to you, Signora.

NINA. I can be found here—or at my house.

MEREDITH. Perhaps we could talk a little now.

NINA. It is not possible now, Monsignore. We have to see the Contessa. Paolo begins work there today. You can talk to him when he is at the villa.

MEREDITH. And you, Signora?

NINA. Whenever you wish. Good-bye, Monsignore—Dottore.
[SHE *starts for the door,* PAOLO *following her*]

[MEYER *doesn't attempt to follow her but goes immediately to* MEREDITH, *who sags against the table. As* MEYER *reaches him,* MEREDITH *gasps and collapses.* MEYER *helps him sit on the couch.* MEREDITH *fumbles for his pillbox.* MEYER *crosses above the sofa to a water pitcher and pours some water from it into a glass and takes it to the couch.* HE *lifts* MEREDITH'S *head as* HE *swallows the pills and sips the water*]

MEREDITH.
[*Still gasping*]
Thank you, Doctor. I hate to be a nuisance.

MEYER. How often is it like this?

MEREDITH. Frequently, now.

MEYER.
 [*Replacing glass on hutch*]
You should be in a hospital.

MEREDITH. Not yet. You must help me stay on my feet as long as possible.

MEYER. I'll try. But I promise no miracle.

MEREDITH. That's what I've been asked to do—pray for a miracle.

MEYER. By whom, Monsignore?

MEREDITH.
 [*Beginning to feel the pain slip away,* HE *sits up, and* MEYER *helps him*]
Thank you, Doctor.

MEYER. By whom?

MEREDITH. The Bishop. Since some of Nerone's reported cures might be miracles, but not provable—he asked me to pray for a sign. A provable miracle.

MEYER. What did you say to that?

MEREDITH. I haven't the courage.

MEYER. Are you afraid of God?

MEREDITH. I'm not sure what I'm afraid of—it's as if I were asked to leap through a paper hoop—on the other side may be darkness or a blinding revelation. All I must do is leap.
 [HE *looks up at* MEYER]
I haven't the courage. Does that seem strange to you, Doctor?

MEYER. Strange from a man like you. But for me, easy to understand.

MEREDITH. Are you also afraid?

MEYER. Yes, all of us here are afraid. The Contessa, Anselmo—we are all involved one way or the other in Nerone's death. None of us came out of it creditably.

MEREDITH. Black?

MEYER. He's afraid you will learn of his fancy for young Paolo.

MEREDITH. That's monstrous.

MEYER. Oh, indeed. Father Anselmo is afraid that you will report to the Bishop that he drinks too much.

MEREDITH. The Bishop knows he drinks.

MEYER. A fine group of sinners, Monsignore?

MEREDITH. Is your only motive for telling me this—truth?

MEYER. Does the motive matter?

MEREDITH. It colors the evidence.

MEYER. So far as any man can be honest about his motives, this is mine. I've made a mess of my life. I had a part in Nerone's death. I was wrong about that. I want to talk it out. Otherwise, like Anselmo, I'll give myself cirrhosis of the liver in order to avoid the nightmares.
[HE *turns to* MEREDITH]
If I couldn't trust you—I couldn't talk to you.

MEREDITH. And what makes you think you can trust me, Doctor?

MEYER.
   [*With a smile*]
Because you have the grace to be ashamed of yourself. That is rare—in or out of the Church.
   [HE *eyes* MEREDITH]
You look better.

MEREDITH. The pain is gone.
   [HE *rises and crosses to the hutch for the water pitcher*]

MEYER. And what now, Monsignore?

MEREDITH.
   [*Crossing to a chair*]
I'd like to talk to you.

MEYER.
   [*Stating a fact*]
About Nerone.

MEREDITH. Yes.

MEYER. Isn't it usual to put on a stole when you hear confessions?

MEREDITH.
   [*Doing so*]
I'll take my shoes off instead.

MEYER. Then I'll tell you as I remember it . . .
   [HE *crosses over to* MEREDITH]
It was summer, the year before the war ended—the young men were gone. I had come here from Rome—an exile in my own land. I tended the sick—for wine—or cheese—or cigarettes. I lived alone because the Calabrese warned me not to touch their pure-blooded women—who, being pure Calabrese, were part Greek, part Phoenician, part French,

Spanish, Italian—anything and everything but Jew. And then one night . . .

> [*As* MEYER *is reaching the end of his speech the* LIGHT PATTERN DIMS *from the warm amber glow of daytime to the cool blue light of night. At the lowest point of the dim,* NINA *and* NERONE *enter and take their places in the side of the set where they will be working. As the* LIGHTS COME UP *to the cool blue pattern,* DR. MEYER *is tending* NERONE's *shoulder.* NINA *is dressed as* SHE *was during this part of the war when* SHE *was younger and happier. When we see* NERONE, HE *is stretched out on the couch in* MEYER's *house.*
>
> [*This pattern of light changes is used in all sequences when we move from the present to the past, and is, of course, reversed when moving back from the past to the present*]

MEYER. Who is he?

NERONE. I can talk for myself.

MEYER. Then, talk.

NERONE. I'm a deserter.

MEYER. What's your name?

NERONE. Giacomo Nerone.

MEYER. What regiment?

NERONE. The 10th Infantry.

MEYER. Where's your uniform?

NERONE. I got rid of it.

MEYER. Where are you from?

NERONE. Reggio.

MEYER. You don't have a Calabrese accent.

NINA. Dottore—he's hurt—he's sick.

MEYER. I can see that—get some water—he's got a bad one.

NINA. Will he feel pain?

MEYER.
   [*Hands her some pills*]
This will help. If anyone finds him here we're as good as
dead.

NINA. Can we throw him out? A sick man?

MEYER. Afterwards. When he's better.

NINA. We will wait till afterwards.

MEYER. You were crazy to bring him here.

NINA. Where could I bring him? To the blacksmith?

MEYER. Nina, after this is done, take him to your house,
make soup and see if he holds it down.

NINA. Will you come to care for him?

MEYER. I cannot come during the day. But at night when
the village is settled down—

NINA. You're a good one, Dottore. In a place full of pigs
you stand up like a man.

MEYER. If the police find out about this—I'll die like a pig.
Put a gag in his mouth.
   [*As* NINA *heads to the couch*]
Anything. And hold him down.

NINA. It's a long time since I've had a man in my arms, Dottore. It'll be a pleasure.

NERONE. I doubt it will be a pleasure.
[*As* MEYER *begins, there is a moan and then* NERONE *struggles and shudders against* NINA *and the gag. As* MEYER *works rapidly and* NERONE *struggles, the* LIGHTS DIM OUT *and* COME UP *again in* MEYER'S *house in the same afternoon pattern of the beginning of the scene with* MEREDITH. NINA *and* NERONE *exit in the dim out.* MEREDITH *is moved by what* HE *has heard.* MEYER *steps into the playing area*]

MEREDITH. And that was the beginning.

MEYER. Yes. Nina fed him well, pawning whatever little she owned for extra food. He survived the wound and my treatment. Then, oh, perhaps two weeks later—
[*Again as* MEYER *finishes his speech the* LIGHT PATTERN DIMS *and changes from amber to blue.* NERONE *and* NINA *enter in the dim and are present when the lights again reveal this second look at the past.* MEYER *has moved into the playing area in his room*]

MEYER.
[*Adjusting the sling that* NERONE *is wearing*]
Each day now—you must begin to use that arm. The muscles will be of no use—unless you begin working them.

NERONE. When will I be strong enough to travel?

MEYER.
[*With a shrug*]
Perhaps three or four weeks. But where do you go?

NERONE. To Rome. Where all my family is—they went there from Reggio.

MEYER. The Allies have landed north of here—and the Germans are moving down. You'll have trouble. There will be questions. Unless you stay in hiding—and then how do you eat?

NINA. I will feed him.

NERONE.
[*With a smile at* NINA]
I'll have to leave your house, Nina.

NINA. Why? There's bed and food. Not much—but better than dying in a ditch with a bullet in you.

MEYER.
[*To* NERONE]
Nerone—during your fevers I've heard you talking in your sleep. You have other loyalties. These might be useful to us later.

NINA.
[*To* MEYER]
What—other loyalties?

NERONE. Giacomo Nerone is an assumed name. My real one is of no importance. I'm English. And now that it's said, forget it.

NINA. English!

MEYER. He said forget it.

NINA. It's forgotten.
[NINA *crosses to him*]
You could stay and work.
[*The* MEN *look at her*]

Yes. There're others—half-a-dozen of them—who have given up the war. Two from here and the others from God knows where. He speaks good Italian—better than me. No one makes a fuss—we're short of men and there's work to be done before winter.

MEYER. Nina—that's too—

NINA. It's not too anything.
[*She looks at* NERONE]
I can get you a job with our foreman, Gozzoli. He lost two sons in the war and hates the Fascisti. When you are better, we will go to him.

NERONE. I'll think about it. It is good of you, Nina. I am grateful. But I have to think about it.
[*To* MEYER]
Thank you, Dottore, for all you've done.
[HE *strolls out of the house, preoccupied and thoughtful.* NINA *starts to follow* NERONE. MEYER *moves toward her and tries to take her in his arms*]

NINA.
[*Moving away and speaking softly*]
No, Dottore.

MEYER. I want you, Nina.

NINA. If you really wanted me—you could have had me long ago. And I'd have been glad. But our time has passed by and you know it.

MEYER.
[*Looking in the direction of* NERONE]
Maybe this time.

NINA. Maybe.

[*As* NINA *exits the* LIGHTS DIM, *then* COME UP AGAIN *in* MEYER'S *house, still in the afternoon light.* MEYER *steps into the playing area near* MEREDITH]

MEYER. Nina was right. Gozzoli gave Nerone a job—and he and Nina became lovers.

MEREDITH. All you know about him was that he was English? And a deserter?

MEYER. Yes. But he didn't behave like a deserter. A deserter is afraid, haunted. He had no fear. Once he was well, he smiled, talked and laughed like a free man.

MEREDITH.
[*Has gone to the hutch for water*]
Did you like him?

MEYER. No. I didn't like him—because I was jealous of him.

MEREDITH. Because of Nina?

MEYER. More than that. I had lived here for years—but had achieved little intimacy with my neighbors. Nerone was at home in a week. The men trusted him. The women loved him. I was still the outsider.

MEREDITH. I know how you felt. I've been like that all my life.
[MEYER *looks at him, wondering if* MEREDITH *means it.* HE *sees that* MEREDITH *does*]
So you were at odds with Nerone?

MEYER. When I didn't see him I disliked him. But when we saw each other—when he'd come to talk or borrow a book—he charmed me.

MEREDITH. Did you talk about many things?

MEYER. Everything. Except Nerone. He was mostly interested in this place—the people, their history—their customs —as if he wanted to take all this in and forget what had belonged to him.

MEREDITH. Did he really care for Nina?

MEYER. They were happy. You could see that.
[HE *stops, turns away to below table*]
For what was between them you'll have to talk to Nina.

MEREDITH. I'm sorry to press you like this, Dottore.

MEYER. I understand. I'm merely trying to keep my evidence first-hand. Then soon it was October. Nerone called me in to examine Nina. She was two months pregnant. They were both very happy about it.

MEREDITH.
[*Returning to his chair*]
Did he make any move to marry her?

MEYER. No. And just when it seemed I had Nerone measured—as a fly-by-night—he surprised me again.

[*The* LIGHTS *in* MEYER's *house* CHANGE *to night—dark night.* MEREDITH *is still pinpointed in a spot but the stage is clear near the door as there is a knock and* NERONE *enters.* HE *is dressed warmly.* HE *carries some books*]

NERONE. Thanks for the books.

MEYER. Help yourself to any others.
[HE *points to his bookcase.* NERONE *places the books* HE *has returned on the bookcase and takes another.* HE *crosses over and faces* MEYER]

NERONE. Thank you. It's going to be a bad winter, Doctor. The harvest was thin, there will be famine. You and I had better start preparing for it now.

MEYER.
[*With a half-shrug*]
How do you prepare for a famine—practice starvation?

NERONE. You and I are the only people around here with ideas or influence. We'll have to create and run an organization.

MEYER. For God's sake, Giacomo—you don't know what you're talking about. You're on the run—I'm a political exile—they'll drop the axe on both our necks.
[HE *makes a chopping gesture*]

NERONE. Who's they, Doctor?

MEYER. The authorities—the police—the Mayor of Gemello Maggiore.

NERONE. All of them are so scared—so interested in saving their own lives—they haven't been around here for weeks. Besides, this is our business—not theirs—we'll handle it ourselves.

MEYER. Handle what?

NERONE. Survival for three months. We will see that everyone gets enough food and fuel to keep alive during the winter. You'll need more medicines— We must find more blankets—we'll set up a central store—ration out supplies—

MEYER. These people are close-fisted when times are good. In famine they'll be like vultures—their families are the only thing that counts—the rest of them can rot in a ditch—

NERONE. We'll teach them the next step—we'll make them
a tribe.

[MEYER *waves a disgusted hand and turns away*]

MEYER. How?

NERONE. Ten families have agreed to put a quarter of their
food stores into a common store for the winter. Every
family is going to try to bring in one more family. Then
you and I, my dear Doctor, will make the rounds and try
to beat some sense into those who are still standing out.

MEYER. I don't see how you did it.

NERONE.
   [*Simply*]
I talked to them. I told them of the soldiers that would be
swarming through here—Italian, German, Allied. I told
them of the house searches when things get bad in the
winter. It took some time and some talking, but in the end
they agreed.

MEYER. I've tried—but I've never been able to do anything
like that.

NERONE. I will have to pay a price for it, of course.

MEYER.
   [*Puzzled*]
What sort of price?

NERONE.
   [*Suddenly somber*]
I don't know yet. But I think it will come very high in
the end.
   [HE *rises*]
Thanks for the book.

[*There is a pause; then* HE *turns and walks out of the house. As* HE *does, the* NIGHT LIGHT PATTERN CHANGES *back into the* AFTER- NOON PATTERN OF LIGHT. MEYER *turns back toward* MEREDITH]

MEREDITH.
[HE *rises*]
Tell me, Dottore—how did the organization work go?

MEYER. It was unbelievable—but it worked. And before the first snows came—we had nearly three tons of supplies sealed up in the Grotta del Fauno.

MEREDITH. The people must have been grateful to Nerone.

MEYER. Very grateful. When the spring came and the sup- plies were gone that's where his friends buried Giacomo.

MEREDITH. And how did that come about, Dottore?

MEYER. Part of that is Nina's story. Perhaps she will tell you tomorrow.
[MEREDITH *nods*]
Up to now, Monsignore—sinner or saint?

MEREDITH. Up to now, Dottore—? Perhaps a bit of each.

MEYER. Ah—a man. Like the rest of us.
[*The* LIGHTS DIM DOWN AND OUT. *For a moment or two the stage is black as the scene ends*]

# Scene III

A T R I S E : *The* LIGHTS ARE UP *in the patio of the* CONTESSA's *villa. On stage is the* CONTESSA, *seated, groomed fastidiously, and a sharp contrast to the slightly disheveled* NINA *who stands near her.* NINA *is standing next to* PAOLO. HE *is uncomfortable and restless. It is late afternoon.*

CONTESSA. I am sure you understand that this is a great opportunity for Paolo?

NINA. It is work. That is good for him. If he works well, it is good for you, too.

CONTESSA.
[*To* PAOLO]
How do you feel about it, Paolo? Are you glad to come?

PAOLO.
[*After a pause*]
I am ready to start work.

CONTESSA. Good.
[*To* NINA]
We haven't discussed wages.

NINA. The Dottore said you would pay what was usual.

CONTESSA. Better than that. Signor Black tells me Paolo is intelligent and willing. I will pay the boy a man's wage.

NINA. Then let it be a man's work.

CONTESSA.
[*Avoiding the barb*]
If he does well—I can do much for him. Help educate him —help him make a career. Perhaps send him to Rome.

NINA. His father was an educated man. He told me one should first educate the heart—then the head.

CONTESSA. How sentimental.
[*Then briskly, anxious to be done with* NINA]
Paolo will live here. He will be home on Sundays.

NINA. I have met Monsignor Meredith. I know he will be seeing Paolo and talking with him.

CONTESSA. The Monsignor is a busy man.

NINA. He is busy with my Giacomo, Signora. And to him, Giacomo's son will be important.

[*The* CONTESSA *rises, indicating this part of the ritual is done.* NINA *bends to pick up a straw basket which* SHE *has been carrying.* SHE *extracts from it a small package and extends it to the* CONTESSA]

My boy is not coming empty-handed to your house. This is a gift.

CONTESSA.

[*Nonplussed by the gesture*]

Thank you.

NINA. We cannot give of our wealth—for we have none. We can only give of our hearts. One day Giacomo may become a "beato"—

[*Hands her the package*]

—and then what you hold will be precious. It is part of the shirt he wore when they killed him. Part of his blood is on it.

[*The* CONTESSA *holds the package as if it were a bomb.* NINA *bows*]

Contessa.

[SHE *turns to go. First* SHE *crosses to* PAOLO, *looks at him, strokes his cheek, then leaves. Slowly, as* PAOLO *watches her, the* CONTESSA *places the package on the table.* SHE *then recovers and faces the boy*]

CONTESSA. Well, Paolo.

PAOLO. Yes, Contessa?

CONTESSA. If you work well for me, you'll never be sorry.

PAOLO. I will try.

CONTESSA. Did you know that I knew your father?
[PAOLO *shakes his head no*]
He used to come here sometimes to visit.
[SHE *moves closer*]
He was my friend. That's why I've brought you here. We
will make you into a gentleman like your father.

PAOLO. I promise to work well.

CONTESSA. Of course you will, Paolo.
[SHE *holds his cheeks and looks into his eyes*]
And you will go to school at Valenta. Learn to read and
write and wear the correct clothes. Then, perhaps, you can
be my friend, too.
[PAOLO *nods, dazed at the future*]

PAOLO. I would like that.

CONTESSA.
[*Holding him tighter and stroking his neck*]
First I must learn to trust you. You must learn to keep
secrets. No gossip—to anyone. Not even the Monsignor—
nor Signor Black.

PAOLO. I promise.

CONTESSA. Nor to your mother.
[PAOLO *nods his promise.* BLACK *enters from the villa and sees
the* CONTESSA *and* PAOLO *together. The* CONTESSA *turns, not at
all nonplussed*]

BLACK. Contessa!

CONTESSA.
[*To* PAOLO]
Go to the gardener, Paolo. He will put you to work and
show you to your room.

BLACK.

> [*As* PAOLO *turns to leave*]

Paolo.

> [PAOLO *stops*]

You didn't greet me.

> [PAOLO *nods a greeting*]

We are friends. I am glad you are here.

PAOLO.

> [*Looking at the* CONTESSA]

I am glad too.

> [HE *leaves*]

BLACK. The boy hasn't lost his milk teeth, cara.

CONTESSA. That's something for you to remember, Nicki.

BLACK.

> [*Putting pad on coffee table*]

Anne—

MEREDITH.

> [*As* HE *enters the patio*]

Good afternoon. Forgive me for being away most of the day. But I'm refreshed and ready to make amends.

CONTESSA. I'm the one to be forgiven. I have a frightful headache—migraine.

> [SHE *picks up the package*]

Please excuse me. I hope I can join you for dinner.

> [SHE *takes the package from the table and leaves.* MEREDITH *watches her leave, then sits down as* BLACK *strolls up to the wall*]

BLACK. How does Dr. Meyer find the state of your health, Monsignore?

MEREDITH. He takes a dim view of my life expectancy.

BLACK. I'm sorry. It would be regrettable if you could not finish your case.

MEREDITH.
[*Ruefully*]
Fortunately the Church is in no hurry. A century or two is neither here nor there.

BLACK. But I have the impression that you're anxious to get through with it.

MEREDITH. The more testimony I can collect now, the better for everybody.

BLACK. Are you afraid of death, Monsignore?

MEREDITH. Who isn't?

BLACK. Many of your colleagues aren't quite so frank about it. Was Dr. Meyer's testimony of any value to you?

MEREDITH. Informative. He is an excellent witness.

BLACK. The Contessa has hired a new worker for her fields. Paolo Sanduzzi.

MEREDITH. I know. I met him at Dr. Meyer's.

BLACK. A charming boy. Pity to see him go to seed in a place like this. Perhaps the Church should do something for him. After all you can't have the son of a saint chasing the girls or getting into trouble with the police—now can you?

MEREDITH.
[*Slowly*]
If the boy is to be corrupted, Mr. Black, you will be the one to do it.

BLACK.

[*With a laugh*]

What else did Meyer tell you about me?

MEREDITH.

Isn't that enough?

[HE *rises*]

What you are doing is a detestable thing. Your private vices are a matter between you and the Almighty. But in trying to corrupt this boy—you are committing a crime against nature—a crime that . . .

BLACK.

[*In hot anger*]

Have you judged me already? You pick up filthy gossip and damn me with it, before you hear a word in my defense.

MEREDITH. If I have misjudged you, Mr. Black, I'm deeply sorry. I'd be happy to hear you deny . . . these rumors.

BLACK. Let's argue on your ground before I defend myself to you.

MEREDITH. Which ground, Mr. Black?

BLACK. Let's say I am what everybody calls me. An unnatural man.

MEREDITH. Yes?

BLACK. What, then, does the Church offer me by way of faith, hope or charity? I've been a Catholic, Monsignore, but I left the Church—because it cannot answer the question I ask you.

MEREDITH. Which question, Mr. Black?

BLACK.
[*Now in control and pressing his argument with conviction on his own logic*]
I'll ask it, and I'll make a bargain. You give me a satisfactory answer and I'll pack and leave here on the first train.

MEREDITH. I won't bargain with you. I'll listen and try to answer.

BLACK.
[*With a laugh*]
All right, then—no bargains. You accuse me of being fond of this boy unnaturally—accuse me of committing a sin against nature. The Church says that the body was made for the procreation of children and then for the commerce of love between man and woman. That's the end?
[MEREDITH *doesn't answer*]
All acts of the body conform to the end and all else is sin.

MEREDITH. The sin is an act in excess of natural instinct.

BLACK. Yes—like lusting for another man's wife—but for me to desire this boy Paolo is a sin against nature—

MEREDITH.
[*Quietly*]
Your knowledge of the sin against nature doesn't make it less contemptible.

BLACK. No, indeed. But here's the catch. What about my nature? I was born the way I am. I was a twin. Hardly identical—
[HE *shakes his head*]
—in no way identical. See my brother before he was lost in the war and you'd have had the perfect male—the exces-

sive male. *That* was his nature. But I knew soon that it was *my* nature to be drawn more to men than to women. I wasn't seduced or blackmailed. It was *my* nature. This is what I am. I can't change it. No one can. I didn't ask to be born like this.

[HE *rises*]

But who made me? According to you—God! He gave me my nature—and what I do, then, is no sin against nature . . .

MEREDITH. Mr. Black—there are degrees of sin—

BLACK. No quick answer, Monsignore. If I were accused of attempting to seduce a girl you'd give me a lecture—you'd disapprove—but I'd be normal. According to nature. But I'm not—built that way.

[MEREDITH *turns to him*]

Somewhere the Almighty slipped a cog in my creation. What do I do—wait until they make me an angel in heaven? I'm lonely. I need love. Do I live in a padded cell till I die?

[*By now* BLACK's *manner has changed from the boasting, logical man of argument to the pleading and rather helpless figure of the guilty.* HE *pauses, trying for composure.* MEREDITH's *manner is no longer accusatory but sympathetic*]

MEREDITH. Mr. Black. There is no answer to your problem —or to a lot of others—that doesn't involve a mystery and an Act of Faith.

[BLACK *turns to answer but* MEREDITH *puts up a hand to quiet him*]

I can't tell you why you are made as you are—any more than I can tell you why I've a carcinoma in my stomach. Or why some other man has a claim to sainthood. Why? Only God knows.

BLACK. If there is a God.

MEREDITH. I'll accept the *if*. If there is no God, then the universe is a chaos with no meaning. Then one lives in it as long and as well as one can—and steals the best of it. But if there is a God—and I believe there is—then—

BLACK. Spare me the rest, Monsignore.
      [*Then angrily and sarcastically*]
I know. No matter what a bloody mess Creation gets into —take it and like it—because that's the bundle you carry— the cross on your back. Take it long enough—and they make a saint of you. That's no answer, Meredith.

MEREDITH. Have you a better one, Mr. Black?

BLACK. Yes. You keep your cross and your hairshirt. I'll give up my stake in Heaven—and take my chances on hell.
      [HE *walks across the patio and into the villa.* MEREDITH *stands in contemplation and wonder as the* LIGHTS DIM OUT *and the scene ends*]


# Scene IV

AT RISE: *The* LIGHTS GO UP *in* NINA's *house. It is a room that includes an earthen oven, the large bed, a heavy table, some old chairs and benches—but all of it, crowded and old, is clean. It is midafternoon.* NINA *is sitting looking up at* MEYER, *who stands near* MEREDITH.

MEYER. I have spoken to the Monsignor and told him up to a point what I know.

NINA. Have you spoken the truth, Dottore?

MEYER. As I knew it. I swear that.

MEREDITH. I believe him, Signora, as I'm sure I will believe you.

NINA. I promised Giacomo I would never tell anyone. Is it a sin if I forget that promise?

MEREDITH. I cannot judge that, Signora, but the Church can never know the full story unless we hear it from you.
[NINA *looks at* MEYER *questioningly.* MEYER *nods his head, indicating that it is better* SHE *tell her story.* NINA *rises and faces* MEREDITH]

NINA. What do you want to ask me, Monsignore?

MEREDITH. Up to now, I know many things—some good, some sinful—about Giacomo. I do not have any indication of his religious belief or of his moral attitude. It is about this I want to know.

MEYER. Now I will leave. Nina's story is her own and it is better if I'm not here.

NINA. It is better.

MEYER.
[*Preparing to go*]
You're a good confessor, Meredith. I like talking with you.

MEREDITH. And you, Doctor, have begun to make me feel close to people. It terrifies me to think how much time I've wasted—and how little there is left.
[*As* MEYER *exits* MEREDITH *turns to* NINA]
Signora, I need to ask you questions. Some may seem strange or brutal. I ask them because I must know everything about Giacomo, good or bad. You understand, Signora?

NINA. Call me by my name, Nina. The Dottore does and you are his friend.

MEREDITH. Thank you. Now, Nina, is it true that you and Giacomo lived together?

NINA. We were lovers. It's not the same thing.

MEREDITH. A while ago I might have frowned rather than smiled. But, my child, you are a Catholic. So was Giacomo. Didn't you think this was a sin against God?

NINA. When you are lonely—and there is fear—and cold—and tomorrow you may not be alive—you can forget about sin.

MEREDITH. Never quite forget! Were your relations normal?

NINA. Normal?

MEREDITH. Well, that is to say—your physical relations—were they—er—

NINA.
[*Proudly*]
Oh, Monsignore—we loved each other. We did what lovers do and were glad of each other.
[*In puzzlement*]
What else could there be?

MEREDITH.
[*Hastily*]
But since you were having his child—and you loved each other—why didn't you marry?

NINA.

[*Impatiently*]

Always the same question. As if it were big and important —but it is only like a wart on a green melon. Monsignore, listen. Tomorrow the police might come or the Germans or the English. We could all die of malaria or the tifo. A ring on the finger means nothing.

MEREDITH. Did Giacomo refuse to marry you?

NINA. I never asked him. You see, Monsignore, I had a husband once. The army took him and he was killed. Now I had a man. If he wanted to go—no ring could keep him. If he was killed—he would also be lost to me. Also, he said that in case of trouble—the child and I would not be punished if we were free. Isn't that clear? Have you never been in love, Monsignore?

MEREDITH. Never, I'm afraid.

[NINA *half-turns away as if that part of the questioning is over*]

Tell me, what sort of man was Giacomo?

NINA.

[*Turning back, her body coming alive under a flock of memories*]

Ah! What sort of man? Oh, Monsignore, he was everything a woman wants. He was strong in bed and yet so gentle. He could be so angry that you trembled—and yet he never lifted his hand or raised his voice. When I served him, he thanked me and was grateful. He could make me laugh—and when he laughed—he was afraid of no one and nothing except that I might be hurt . . . That sort of man. . . .

MEREDITH. Yes—I see.

NINA. Did the Dottore tell you why Giacomo gave up the war?

[MEREDITH *shakes his head*]

He told us about it one day in the winter—it was a cold and hard time. Everyone locked themselves in from the cold. If there was a knock at the door we knew it was a brigand or a crazy man and we did not answer. But they opened their doors to my Giacomo because he came to help them with food or medicine. That night Meyer was here to help me because I had a fever and my Giacomo came home. . . .

[*The* LIGHTS ARE CHANGING *to a* PATTERN OF A COLD NIGHT. MERE-DITH, *seated to one side, watches intently. When the lights are fixed we see* NINA *sitting on the bed.* MEYER *is standing next to her, having concluded an examination. There is a sharp rap on the door and a low whistle.* NERONE *staggers in.* HE *wears a knapsack over his ragged and bulky garments. His boots are covered with sacking.* NERONE *wearily slips the knapsack from his shoulder, and goes to* NINA]

NERONE. How is my Nina?

MEYER. Her fever will pass. She will not lose the baby.

NINA. Your Nina is stronger than you. You will fall in the snow one night and freeze to death.

MEYER. She's right, you know. You're pressing yourself too hard.

NERONE. There is so much to do.

NINA.

[*Crossing to the stove and preparing some food*]

And if you keep on—none of it will be done. Giacomo mio, stop—I beg of you.

NERONE. I cannot.

MEYER. Cannot—why not?

NERONE.
> [*Pouring himself some wine*]

I must work—as hard as I possibly can. I hope it will bring me some comfort and peace.

MEYER. If you are using work like a drug—I've got things that will do the job faster.

NINA. Caro mio, can I help?

NERONE. You have been good, carissima, and dear.
> [*Then* HE *looks at* MEYER *and nods his head*]

And I am grateful to you. It is time I told you both why I came here.

MEYER. You don't have to.

NERONE. I need to.
> [HE *pushes the food away*]

Nina, cara, the food must wait.
> [*Obediently,* NINA *returns the food to the stove*]

NERONE. I was in the advance attack on Messina. My company was assigned to clean out a block of tenements leading down to the docks. There were some scattered snipers— a couple of machine guns—nothing much.

NINA. I don't want to hear. I don't know what it is—but I don't want to hear.

NERONE.
> [*Paying no attention to* NINA]

We came to a blind alley with windows facing us and a sniper in the top window. Then we thought we had finished him—we moved in. When we got to the house—I shouted a

surrender warning. From a lower window there was another shot—and one of my men went down. I pitched a
grenade through the window, and after the burst went in.
I found the sniper. An old fisherman, with a woman and a
nursing child. All dead. The baby had taken the full
burst. . . .
  [NINA *moans in sympathy*]

MEYER. It happens in war. It's the human element.

NERONE. But I was the human element. So my war was over.
I ran away.

MEYER. Why did you come here?

NERONE. I don't know. Call it an accident. Aldo—I know
about Nina—but not about you. Do you believe in God?

MEYER. The Fascisti have done their best to persuade me
that there is none—let's say I have an open mind in the
matter.
  [*Then quickly* HE *points a finger*]
Giacomo—do you believe in God?

NERONE. I used to. Then for a long time I didn't.
  [HE *turns and looks at* NINA—*and holds her hand*]
Nina, you are my refuge. I want to believe our child will
bring a new life to replace the one I destroyed. Then, Aldo,
when we started doing something for all these people, perhaps that was my reparation to the dead fisherman and dead
woman . . . but it isn't enough.

MEYER. It never is. But where does God come in?

NERONE. With God everything is important—every life—
every death. . . . And the reparation means nothing un-

less you give yourself as part of it. Do you understand,
cara mia?

NINA. I will try to if you ask me, Giacomo.

MEYER. My friend. Let me give you some medical advice.
[*Picks up his bag from bed*]
You're ragged with fatigue and undernourishment. And all
this doubt is part of your fatigue. Stay home a few days—
let Nina love you and feed you. You two take care of each
other.
[MEYER *exits*]

NINA. Rest, Giacomo, rest . . .

NERONE. Nina, come here.
[NINA *crosses to him and* HE *holds her*]
Sometimes a man does a thing and his woman hates him.

NINA. I know. But I could never hate you.

NERONE. Whatever I did, you would still love me?

NINA. Always.

NERONE. Then sit here and listen to me. . . . I was born
and raised in the country. I lived with my family and
learned something about love and about God from the
place in which I lived. Then, Nina, I became lost—for a long
time—and when I saw the mangled body of that baby in
Messina I thought I was lost forever. You see, once I knew
I came from God and would go back to Him. I could do
wrong and be forgiven. But then I became lost. And I am
still walking in the mist—looking for the road back to God.
I am still uncertain where I came from and where I am
going and what I should do. Faith is a comfort and a

burden. Without realizing it, I began to rid myself of the burden—I thought I'd feel free. I had no question of conscience—then slowly I knew that by ridding myself of the burden—I had also lost the comfort. Suddenly I felt terror— I needed the comfort of Faith, but I could not find it. I knew then that Faith was a gift of God—the comfort and the burden. . . . Nina, am I talking like a crazy man?

NINA.

[*Puzzled but eager to understand*]
You are talking with love and my heart understands.

NERONE. Will you try to understand what I am going to ask you?

NINA. When you hold me like this and I can feel the love in your hands and in your voice, I understand everything.

NERONE. Then, Nina—when the spring comes and life is easier, I have to leave you—go away for a while.

NINA. No, caro mio, no!

NERONE. Not from this valley. From this house.

NINA. Why? Why?

NERONE. I must find a secret place. Build it, if I must, with my own hands. I want to live there alone with God. I want to say, "I am lost. If You are there, speak to me clearly. Show me who I am and where I am going." I must do this, cara.

NINA. And what about the child and—me?

NERONE. I will be here all the time. I will see you often. God, if he knows anything, knows I love you.

NINA. And yet you go away?

NERONE. There is love in this, too, Nina—more than you know. For this is the reason. With spring the armies will be moving. First the Germans—and then the partisans to bother the Germans—and then the Allies, who will push them back. Some or all of them will come in turn to Gemello. I will be known because of what I do for the people. If I am lucky, they will accept me and I can help some more. If I am not lucky—I may be taken and killed.

NINA. Dio! No!

NERONE. Nina, it may be this is what lies behind the mists and that I will see at one time the face of God and the face of the executioners. You cannot be involved. If I am taken, Meyer will look after you. If all falls well, we'll be married and the child will have my name.

NINA. I will suffer when you are not here.

NERONE. Less that way than the other.

NINA. Hold me, caro mio! Hold me, I'm afraid.

NERONE. Lie here on my arm, carissima. I'm here and you can sleep safe.

NINA.
[*Tearfully*]
Now perhaps—but when you are gone?

NERONE. I shall never be gone, carissima, never, till eternity.
[*The* LIGHTS GO DIM *again, and as they change,* NERONE *exits. The* AFTERNOON EFFECT RETURNS. MEREDITH *is moved by what* HE *has heard.* HE *hesitates a moment, as* NINA *regains her composure*]

MEREDITH.

[*Softly*]

Nina, my child, when did he leave you?

NINA. In the early spring.

MEREDITH. And when he left, what then?

NINA. He went into the valley and lived in a cave and built his hut. But he still traveled the valley, working for those who could not work—looking after the sick—

MEREDITH. Did you see him during this time?

NINA. Every day—as he promised.

MEREDITH. Was he changed?

NINA. Only that he was more gentle and more careful of me.

MEREDITH. This question must be asked. Did he make love to you?

NINA.

[*Simply*]

I was big with child, Monsignore. I was calm and content. So was Giacomo.

[*A pause*]

One day—a Saturday—the Germans had arrived and they made their headquarters in the Contessa's villa. In the evening Giacomo had come to see me and the Dottore came to say good-bye . . .

MEREDITH. Good-bye?

[NINA *nods and, as the* LIGHTS CHANGE, NINA *moves into the playing area near the bed, where* MEYER *and* NERONE *have already moved during the light change*]

MEYER.

[*Placing a knapsack and his doctor's bag on the table*]
I'm pulling out.

NINA. Why? You will be safe.

MEYER. No. I won't. The Germans will learn quickly enough there's a Jew here and I'll be shipped north to a concentration camp.
[HE *turns to* NERONE]
I'm taking my instruments and some drugs—but I've left you a stock in the big box under my bed.

NERONE. Where are you going, Aldo?

MEYER. East, to a partisan hideout. I've been in contact with them.
[NINA *meanwhile is busying herself preparing some cheese, bread and coffee which* SHE *is placing in* MEYER'S *knapsack*]
Their leader is a man named Il Lupo. He has the look of a trained man.

NERONE. He should. He's a professional, trained in Russia.

MEYER. He has guns, ammunition and good communications. When you need me . . .
[*He points to* NINA, *meaning if* SHE *also needs him*]
. . . go out along the San Bernardino road about ten kilometers, then turn off at Satan's Rock. That's where the sentries are. Climb to the top of the rock, light a cigarette, take out your handkerchief and knot it around your neck.

NERONE. How about singing *God Save the King?*

MEYER. Remember what I told you. You could be shot if you forget.
[NINA *continues packing food for* MEYER *into his knapsack*]

Nina, tell Giacomo to come with me.
[*To* NERONE]
The Germans could shoot you as a spy.

NERONE. I know the Germans better than you do.

MEYER. Nina—are you happy with this—this arrangement?

NINA. There was never another man like Giacomo.

MEYER. You know what he does up there in his hut?

NINA. I know. He prays. He thinks. He works the garden.

MEYER. I may as well get this off my mind. The other night,
Giacomo, I went up to see you. You were on your knees
on the floor, praying with your eyes closed and your hands
stretched out. I spoke to you—and you didn't hear me.
[HE *goes toward* NERONE]
I went up to you and shook you! You were rigid! I
couldn't budge you! You hear me now?
[NERONE *nods*]
Then I went away. This prayer business is all right, I sup-
pose—but you can go crazy with too much of it!

NERONE. Do you think I'm crazy?

MEYER. I didn't say that. Strange, that's all.

NINA. Maybe, Dottore, there aren't many good men around.
We forget what they look like.

MEYER.
[*His anger leaves him.* HE *takes his knapsack and doctor's bag*]
That could be so. Thanks for the food. Remember, Gia-
como, how to reach me.

NINA.

[*Going to* MEYER *and kissing his cheek*]
Good luck, Dottore!

MEYER. Maybe we all deserve some.
[HE *goes to the door and exits*]

NERONE. Go with God, Aldo.
[NINA *and* NERONE *look at each other*]
Aldo's been waiting a long time for his own war.
[HE *shakes his head*]
But Aldo doesn't know that Il Lupo won't help him fight
it. He wants Meyer so that he can use him after he's helped
bring Communism to Italy.
[HE *gestures with his hands*]
Then poor Aldo will be squeezed—like a grape.
[HE *goes to* NINA *and holds her gently and tenderly*]
But we will try to do our work here.

NINA. What will you do, Giacomo?

NERONE. Knowing that the Germans would be here—I went
to see the Contessa two days ago.
[NINA *moves away from his arms*]

NINA. I do not want you to see the Contessa.

NERONE. It was necessary. I told her I was English.

NINA.

[*Furious and jealous*]
She will turn you in.

NERONE. No. I told her I was an agent—working with the
Allies. She agreed to let me act as her steward so that I can
talk to the Germans.

NINA. But you'll be staying at the villa.

NERONE. Only when I must. The German officers will be quartered at the villa.

NINA. Then the Contessa can have a new man every night.

NERONE. Carissima. Don't say that. The Contessa is a sad, lonely woman—with a fire that no one has been able to put out.

NINA. Ah! That's a joke!

NERONE. No, Nina, that's a torment.

NINA. She is no good!
   [SHE *spits*]
Let the fire she has—burn her up.

NERONE.
   [*Imitating her with humor*]
She is no good!
   [HE *imitates the gesture of contempt* NINA *has made and also the slight spitting gesture* SHE *has made. Then* HE *laughs.* NINA *looks at him—then laughs and runs into his arms. As* THEY *embrace the* LIGHTS DIM *and when they come back to the* AFTERNOON PATTERN NINA *stands facing* MEREDITH. NERONE *has exited*]

NINA.
   [*Seated on bench*]
So I forgot my fear and hate of the Contessa—and spent what hours I could listening to Giacomo and loving him for his faith and his kindness.

MEREDITH. My child—did Giacomo during this time—go to Mass and the Sacraments?

NINA. Yes.

MEREDITH. Did he go to Confession?

[SHE *nods*]

When was your son born?

NINA. In May.

[SHE *pauses*]

When the hard pains came, Giacomo ran to Satan's Rock for Meyer.

[*As* SHE *has been speaking, the* LIGHTS DIM OUT *and go to a* NIGHT PATTERN. *During the change,* NINA *gets into bed.* NERONE *and* MEYER *enter and take positions near the bed.* NERONE *has the* CHILD *wrapped in a blanket as the* LIGHTS COME UP. MEYER *stands at the foot of the bed.* NINA *is moaning softly with after-pain of birth*]

MEYER. He's a solid boy and all of him is there.

NERONE. Look at him. He has the face of a good man.

[MEYER *has crossed and peered at the* BABY, *smiling. Suddenly he frowns—then examines the* CHILD *more closely.* MEYER *crosses to the table with the* BABY *and* NERONE *follows.* HE *examines the* INFANT *near the light. The examination is tense.* HE *whispers to* NERONE. NERONE *looks. Again a whisper.* NINA *is aware of the whispering.* SHE *lifts her head from the pillow*]

NINA. What's wrong?

[*The* MEN *do not answer*]

What's the matter with the baby? Tell me, caro mio, tell me. Dottore! Please!

MEYER.

[*To* NERONE]

Tell her.

NERONE.

[*Goes to the bed above and speaks gently*]

He's blind, cara.

[NINA *moans in shock*]

He was born with cataracts. Aldo says it was the fever you had—the illness with the spots.

> [NINA's *moans now turn into a scream.* SHE *screams again and then buries her face in the pillow.* MEYER *prepares a syringe and crosses to her*]

NINA. Let me die! I am ashamed. I've given my man a blind child!

NERONE. I love him. I love you, carissima.

> [HE *holds her and the sobs rack her body.* NERONE *strokes her hair and nods to* MEYER, *who applies the hypodermic to* NINA's *arm*]

MEYER.

> [*Softly*]

This is a sad thing, Nina, but it has happened and for the present it cannot be altered. After the war—we will go to Naples and find a specialist. Now we must wait.

NINA. He's blind—he's blind.

NERONE. Then we must love him even more.

MEYER. And he must be fed.

> [MEYER *takes the* CHILD *from the crib and hands the* BABY *to* NINA. SHE *holds the* BABY *to her bosom under the covers.* MEYER *crosses to the center of the room*]

Soon she will sleep. She's strong. In a few days she will begin to live for him. . . . I'll be here in the morning.

> [HE *kisses her forehead*]

Giacomo—get some rest yourself.

> [MEYER *goes to the door and exits*]

NERONE. Rest, carissima. You won't be alone tonight. I'll be here with both of you.

> [*Softly* HE *hums an Italian folk song. Halfway through it* HE *stops.* HE *goes to the lamp and lowers it.* HE *stands full height, then unselfconsciously* HE *kneels to the floor. His eyes close*

*and his lips move in silent prayer. His arms go out, like the arms of a cross. His body becomes rigid and* HE *appears transfixed in prayer and concentration.* NINA, *half-lifting her head from the pillow, calls to him*]

NINA. Giacomo! Giacomo!
[HE *doesn't hear her.* SHE *moans softly and settles her head on the pillow. The* LIGHTS HOLD *on the picture of* NERONE *on the floor,* THEN IRIS OUT. NERONE *exits as the stage goes black. During the blackout,* NINA *gets out of bed and when the* LIGHTS COME BACK UP *to the* AFTERNOON PATTERN *of light,* SHE *is standing facing* MEREDITH]

NINA. When the morning light came and I woke up, Giacomo told me to name the boy Paolo, for the Apostle who was blind, but who saw again through the mercy of God. And Giacomo said to me—in three weeks our Paolo would see—the cataracts would disappear.
[*Then with pride and triumph*]
And, Monsignore—three weeks to the day and the hour— I held my son to the light. His eyes were clear and shining like his father's and he blinked at the light.
[*A pause*]
Do you believe what I have told you, Monsignore?

MEREDITH. Yes, Nina. I do believe you.
[NINA *nods happily*]
What did Giacomo say?

NINA. By then, Monsignore—he was dead.
[MEREDITH *lowers his head.* NINA *crosses to the bed. From under the mattress she takes a folder of papers that have been wrapped in oilcloth. Slowly* SHE *crosses back to* MEREDITH]
Now that I have told you what I know, I want you to have these papers Giacomo wrote. They are all that is left of him.

MEREDITH. Thank you, Nina. These are important. When did he write them?

NINA. During the time he lived at the hut. The night before he died he gave them to me.

MEREDITH. Have you read them?

NINA. No. He wrote them in English, which I cannot read. Will you, Monsignore, protect Giacomo's son and keep him safe from the painter?

MEREDITH. Yes. I'll try.
[*Suddenly* MEREDITH *is hit with a piercing shaft of pain.* HE *clutches his body.* NINA, *alarmed, goes to him*]

NINA. Monsignore—

MEREDITH.
[*In agony*]
Please, Nina, call Dr. Meyer.
[MEREDITH *staggers with pain as* NINA *rushes out.* GIACOMO's *papers fall from his hands.* HE *clutches at his body and then, suddenly stabbed by a sharp pain,* HE *almost screams*]
Oh God!
[HE *now turns and his eyes go toward the heavens. Through pain,* MEREDITH *reaches the moment of submission.* HE *drops to his knees*]
Take me, oh God—make me what You will—a wonder or a mockery—
[HE *winces sharply and then moves from agony into quiet resignation, and his words come softly*]
But before You take me, help me save the boy for his father's sake.

*End of Act II*

# ACT 3

# Scene I

AT RISE : *It is evening in* MEYER's *home. The lamps are lit. The stage is bare for half a moment. Then* MEYER *enters from his examination room.* HE *looks back at the room, frowns, then crosses to his pipe and tobacco.* MEREDITH *enters from the examination room, making final adjustments to the buttons of his soutane.* MEYER *is packing his pipe as* MEREDITH *eyes him.*

MEREDITH. You're an outspoken man, Aldo—
     [*Urgently and soberly*]
Go on—speak out.

MEYER. You haven't much time, my friend.

MEREDITH. How much?

MEYER. I don't know. I should get in touch with the Bishop and have you hospitalized.

MEREDITH. I need a few more days.

MEYER. You're a very sick man. Why burn yourself out?

MEREDITH. Better to burn out than rust out.
     [MEYER *nods*]
May I stay for a while?

MEYER. You'd better.

MEREDITH. I'd like to check a couple of points about Nina's story.

MEYER. Ask what you like.

MEREDITH. Was there an outbreak of German measles here in the winter of 1943?

MEYER. Yes—and in answer to your next question—Paolo Sanduzzi was born blind because of it.

MEREDITH. Then you can guess my next question.

MEYER. Yes—when I saw him almost four years later—the cataracts *had* disappeared.

MEREDITH. Four years later?

MEYER.
   [*With a nod*]
After Nerone's death, I went to Rome for that time—then I returned here—because I felt displaced I came back to Gemello Minore to try again—to win some of their hearts— some of their minds.
   [HE *pauses, waves a disgusted hand and rises*]
I came back because I belonged here—no place else.

MEREDITH. I understand. Tell me, Aldo, was the case of Paolo strange—unique?

MEYER. Abnormal. I never heard of another such case.

MEREDITH. Did you discuss it with Nina?

MEYER. Of course—she just shrugged when I asked her about it—and said—the way the peasants do—"It just happened"—

MEREDITH. Nina told me it was a miracle promised by Nerone—that the cataracts disappeared when he said they would. Three weeks after the boy's birth.

MEYER. I can't say what you'd like me to say. I don't believe in miracles, only in unexplained facts. A case like this doesn't normally happen. I've never heard of one and I don't have any medical explanation. Someone else might.

MEREDITH. If they could, could they explain Nerone's fore-knowledge of the cure?

MEYER. Probably if they could explain one, they could explain the other.
[HE *smiles*]
I'm of little use to you.

MEREDITH. But you do accept the truth of Nina's report?

MEYER. I do.

MEREDITH. And you would so testify at the Bishop's Court?

MEYER.
[*Raising his hand as if already taking the oath*]
I would.
[MEREDITH *smiles*]
Now, Monsignore—what's your own opinion? Not for the Bishop's Court—

MEREDITH
[*Serious again*]
I shall try to argue and have my successor argue that this is not a miracle—but simply a rare physical phenomenon. Since it rests on only one witness and your later testimony—the Court will probably refuse to accept it as a miracle—though

in fact it may be one. You see, Aldo, we differ in that you reject the possibility of miracles and I accept it.

MEYER. It's like the two men who were lost in the desert. One of them was convinced there was water fifty miles away—the other didn't believe it. They both died of thirst anyway.

[MEREDITH *laughs*]

MEREDITH. Then let's get to something more provable.

MEYER. I'm ready.

MEREDITH. Tell me about Il Lupo. And how did he become involved with Nerone?

MEYER. Il Lupo wanted to meet Nerone, so I arranged for them to be here late one night. . . .

[*As* HE *clears the playing area, the scene changes, leaving* MEREDITH *seated listening to* MEYER. *As* MEYER *talks, the* LIGHTS CHANGE THEIR PATTERN *and when the* LIGHTS GO UP, IL LUPO, *a lean, clean-shaven leader of the Partisans, is in the room. With him is* NERONE *and* TWO *of* IL LUPO'S PARTISANS]

IL LUPO.

[*To* NERONE]

Happy to know you.

[THEY *shake hands*]

I've heard much about you. I'm sorry about your baby—very sad.

NERONE. Thank you for your sympathy.

IL LUPO. Meyer tells me the mother had rubella—see—that's where a state medical service could be such help. You can start inoculations at the beginning of an outbreak. You had no serum, of course?

MEYER. No.

IL LUPO. It's very sad. Let's hope for the best—maybe later the boy can be helped.

NERONE. I pray he can.

IL LUPO. Yes—I know all about you.

NERONE. All?

IL LUPO. All I need to know. You're English—an officer—a deserter.

NERONE. Right.

IL LUPO. It means nothing to us. The Allied armies have served a purpose by helping to win the war.
[*Foot up on chair*]
Now it is up to us to establish the peace. So your personal history is no worry—it could even help you—with us.
[HE *cleans some mud off his boots with the tip of his bayonet*]
Meyer has told me of your work in Gemello. All that's very good—as a temporary measure.

NERONE. Why temporary?

IL LUPO. Because when the war ends—as it will soon—this country will need a strong and united government to organize and run it.

NERONE. You're saying it will be a Communist government?

IL LUPO. Yes. We are the only ones with a clear platform and we're strong enough to put it into practice.
[HE *replaces his bayonet*]

NERONE. And you are asking me to join the ranks?

IL LUPO. As has your friend Meyer.

> [NERONE *looks at* MEYER]

He is the wise one who has seen the failure of liberalism. People under hard times are stupid and selfish; therefore they need the discipline of power. Take yourself. Here you are acting like Saint Antonio with a basket of eggs—but stand in the way of additional benefits to your people of Gemello and they'll walk over you. There's no future for you, Nerone.

NERONE. No future.

IL LUPO. We are beginning to move into the villages one by one—setting up our own offices. Gemello is next. What are you going to do?

NERONE. I could rally the people and fight you.

IL LUPO. We'd cut you up in an hour. We've got the bullets.

NERONE. I know. The people will be told to wait it out without violence until the first free election.

IL LUPO. By then—they'll forget the guns. They'll remember only the bread and pasta and chocolate they'll get from us.

NERONE.

> [*For the first time* HE *becomes angry*]

They will also remember the boys you've shot in the ditches. The old men beaten and the girls with shaved heads.

IL LUPO.

> [*Quietly*]

You'll have to leave Gemello.

NERONE. You're too greedy. You want me running from my people like a rabbit while you march in as their savior.

IL LUPO. If you stay I'll have to kill you.

NERONE. Yes.

IL LUPO. You want to make yourself a martyr, is that it?

NERONE. That would be foolish and presumptuous. I don't want to die. But I live on land that I've tilled with my hands, in a place where I have found love and hope and belief. I won't be rooted out of it to give you a cheap victory.

IL LUPO. Good. Now we know where we stand.

NERONE. Yes.

MEYER. Il Lupo, Nerone has the confidence of the people. He can do a lot of good—and wants to do no harm. Why not let him be?

IL LUPO. Save your breath, Meyer. He wants no friends.

NERONE. You're wrong. I want Meyer's friendship.

IL LUPO.
    [*To* MEYER]
We'll be taking over Gemello in two days. You've got that long to talk sense into your friend Nerone. Otherwise I told you what would happen. That's all. Good-bye, Nerone.

NERONE. Good-bye.
    [IL LUPO *and the* PARTISANS *exit*]

MEYER. Giacomo—I'm with Il Lupo because it is a natural thing. I haven't joined any party. But I see no reason for you to be hurt.

NERONE. What are Il Lupo's plans for me?

MEYER. You're to be discredited and—then executed.

NERONE. What are Il Lupo's plans for me?

MEYER. You'll be arrested about nine o'clock Thursday morning and brought here for summary trial.

NERONE. Then?

MEYER. You'll be sentenced—then publicly executed.

NERONE. How?

MEYER. A firing squad. This will be a military court. Il Lupo is careful about the formalities.

NERONE. And Nina and the boy?

MEYER. They'll be safe—Il Lupo sees no benefit in punishing them—it might raise sympathy.

NERONE. He thinks of everything.

MEYER.
   [*Pleading*]
Giacomo—you've got almost forty-eight hours to clear out. I've got enough money to keep Nina and the baby for two months. It's yours if you're out of here by sunrise.

NERONE. No. I'm staying.

MEYER. Then what's to be said?

NERONE. Nothing. I'm grateful you tried.

MEYER. Where will you be at nine o'clock Thursday morning?

NERONE. I'll come here.

MEYER. That won't please Il Lupo. He wants a public arrest.

NERONE. He can't have everything. At nine o'clock I'll walk in here on my own. I'll go to Father Anselmo and ask him to hear my confession—then I'll go to the villa and ask the Contessa to take Nina and the boy until this is over.

MEYER. I'm sorry it will end like this.

NERONE. Don't be. You know, it isn't every man who knows the time and place of his death. And, Aldo, I believe that this is the way it is intended to be.
> [*The* LIGHTS FADE. NERONE *exits during the change and the* LIGHTS COME UP *as they were before.* MEREDITH *and* MEYER *are again facing each other*]

MEYER. I heard later that Father Anselmo refused to hear his confession. As you know, he didn't like Nerone.

MEREDITH. Did the Contessa give Nina and the child refuge?

MEYER. No.

MEREDITH. Did Nerone tell you why not?

MEYER. No. Because Thursday morning, Nerone was arrested at Nina's house an hour after sunrise.

MEREDITH. How did Il Lupo know he was there?

MEYER. I never asked.

MEREDITH. Perhaps someone betrayed him.

MEYER. Perhaps. Or Il Lupo might have made a lucky guess.

MEREDITH. Do you believe he was deliberately waiting for martyrdom?

MEYER. No—no—it was more as if he were refusing to escape from it. Is there a difference?

MEREDITH. I think there is. Tell me about the trial.

MEYER. It was a farce. After they trapped him—they beat him up to make it look as though he had resisted them— then they marched him through the street to my house—
> [MEREDITH *has now moved from the couch down front and* MEYER, *talking to him, is also front as the* LIGHTS CHANGE. *When the* LIGHTS TAKE ON THE PATTERN *for the scene,* IL LUPO *is seen at the table—*THREE GUARDS *are stationed around the room—* NERONE, *his face bloodied, his hands and arms cramped from being bound and his shirt torn, stands in front of the table.* MEYER *has left* MEREDITH *standing*]

IL LUPO. Nerone, you shouldn't have tried to run away. . . . You must have. Or else we wouldn't have been so rough with you.
> [HE *picks up a paper*]
Giacomo Nerone, you are charged before this military court with desertion from the British Army and with active collaboration with German units operating in the area of Gemello Maggiore and Gemello Minore.
> [HE *places the paper down*]
Before you go to trial on these charges—you can make a statement.

NERONE. Very well. On the charge of desertion—this court has no jurisdiction. Only a British court martial can try me. You should hand me over to the nearest British command.

IL LUPO. It's a good point. So we forget that one. But you will still be brought to trial on the second charge.

NERONE. I challenge your jurisdiction on that, too.

IL LUPO. On what grounds?

NERONE. This is not a proper court. Your officials hold no legal commission.

IL LUPO. We support the others. We have a de facto identity as military units and therefore summary jurisdiction in all local areas of war. Our authority derives from the Allied High Command. It says that in this paper.

NERONE. I have nothing more to say.

IL LUPO. We want to see that justice is done. We will give you some time to prepare your defense. Doctor Meyer will act as your defense counsel. We will give full consideration to any points you raise. Clear?

NERONE. Quite clear. May I have some coffee, Aldo— please?

> [IL LUPO *dismisses the* GUARDS *and* THEY *exit. In a moment* HE *and* NERONE *and* MEYER *are alone*]

IL LUPO. You were a fool to stay.

NERONE. It's done.

IL LUPO. I have much admiration for you. But I don't see you acting the part of a martyr.

NERONE. You put me into it.

IL LUPO. You accepted. Why?

NERONE.
[*With a smile*]
Let's say I like the part.
[MEYER *hands him a cup of coffee*]

IL LUPO. You like the part—and the "work"?

NERONE. The work isn't important. A million men can do it better. Maybe you, yourself. The work dies. How many men did Christ cure? How many are alive today? The work is an expression of what a man is, feels and believes. If it lasts—and develops—it's not because of the man who began it but because other men think, feel and believe the same way. Your party's an example. You'll die, too, you know. What then?

IL LUPO. The work will go on. The old systems will die. But the people will come into their own. Maybe I won't be here to see it—but I'm not important.

NERONE. That's the difference. You say you're not important. I say I am—because I was from eternity in the mind of God—me—the blind, the futile, the famishing; every single me. I was, I am, I shall be.

IL LUPO. You believe that?

NERONE. I do.

IL LUPO. You'll die for it?

NERONE. Yes.

IL LUPO. You're a fanatic. It's insanity.

NERONE. It's gone on for thousands of years. I wonder will yours last so long?

IL LUPO. Your trial begins at one o'clock. How are you going to plead?

NERONE. Does it matter?

IL LUPO. No. The execution is fixed for three o'clock. Less chance for demonstration. By the time they stop talking and begin to think about it—it's time for supper.

MEYER. Giacomo, if you want to be alone—use that room. No one will disturb you.

NERONE. Thank you, Aldo.
> [THEY *embrace*]
You've been a good friend. I'll remember you.
> [NERONE *exits*]

IL LUPO.
> [*Seeing* MEYER'*s disaffection*]
I'll let you go after the execution. If you take my advice you'll cut loose, and go away for a while. You're not made for this sort of business.

MEYER. I know. I don't believe enough.
> [IL LUPO *exits.* MEYER *rises as the* LIGHTS MOVE HALF BACK *to the present and remain half in the past. So* MEYER'*s next speech gives us a sense of his being suspended between his memories and the action of the moment*]
Later, after the trial, he was marched out. I stayed here alone. I heard the shuffle of the boots—
> [HE *hears it but we do not*]
—then the faint sound of command—
> [HE *hears it but we do not*]
—and finally—

[HE *hears the sharp crackling sound of the volley from the rifles of the firing squad and shudders at the memory*

[*Now the* LIGHTS CHANGE *to as they were between* MEREDITH *and* MEYER. MEYER *stands as* HE *was when* HE *heard the shots*]
—it was done.

MEREDITH. Did Nina see it happen?

MEYER. Yes—then I helped her wash him—dress him—and bury him. Some of the firing squad who knew Giacomo were with us—Martino—Rossi—and others.

MEREDITH. Why were they with Il Lupo?

MEYER. Because they believed in him and in what he said he could do for them. First they loved Giacomo—then when he stood in the way of what they wanted, they hated him— then when he was dead—I guess they could love him again.

MEREDITH. Love can be a terrible thing.

MEYER. Or, beautiful.

MEREDITH. What, Aldo—makes the difference? And what makes us learn to love?

MEYER. Need—I suppose. People needing something—
   [*Before* MEREDITH *can answer there is a knock on the door and* MEYER *crosses to it*]

NINA.
   [*As* SHE *enters, pushing* PAOLO]
Excusate. I know it is late. But this is important.
   [SHE *beckons to* PAOLO]
I want him to tell you what he told me.

MEYER. What is it, Paolo?
   [PAOLO *doesn't answer*]

NINA. He came from the villa. He was happy.

[SHE *looks at him*]

Tell the Dottore why you are so happy.

PAOLO. The Contessa told me I'm going to Rome. She wants to train me to read and write and be a gentleman.

MEYER. Wait. Who's going to Rome?

PAOLO. The Contessa. And she's taking me. She's going to see her doctor and we are to be there for two months.

NINA. Tell him, Dottore—he cannot do this.

MEYER. What your mother is afraid of—is that in Rome, there will be other people with the Contessa.

PAOLO.

[*Sharply*]

It isn't like that. She said the English painter is staying here.

NINA. For how long? A week? Ten days? Then he'll pack and go to Rome for you.

[SHE *shakes her head*]

You cannot go. I am your mother and I say no.

PAOLO. Then I'll go anyway.

MEREDITH. When you're a man and can pay your own way —you can talk like that, Paolo.

NINA. Don't be so patient, Monsignore.

[SHE *pulls* PAOLO *up*]

Listen to me. If there is any nonsense, we will get in touch with the police. That will keep the Contessa and the Englishman quiet. Now forget it.

[SHE *takes the boy's arm*]

PAOLO.

[*Wrenching free*]

I won't forget it. I won't. She asked me and I want to go. She's the padrona and you're nobody—you're just—a saint's whore.

[MEYER *swings his hand sharply at* PAOLO's *face.* PAOLO *staggers, then holds his face and, crying, runs out*]

MEYER.

[*To* NINA]

He didn't mean it, Nina. He's a boy.

NINA. Excuse, Dottore—I will go after him.

[*Then in a desperate appeal*]

Monsignore—he needs help.

MEREDITH. Aldo, please, will you drive me to the villa?

[*The* LIGHTS DIM AS *the scene ends*]


# Scene II


*The* LIGHTS COME UP *in the* CONTESSA's *villa. It is late that evening.*

A T  R I S E : SHE *is revealed sitting in a chair reading an Italian newspaper.* SHE *looks up with annoyance as* BLACK *comes in.* HE *is dressed in his dinner clothes and* HE *is quite drunk.*

BLACK.

[*Singing boisterously*]

Oh, the Queen of Spain was an amorous dame, a lascivious dame was she, and she longed to fool with . . .

CONTESSA. Nicki, where have you been?

BLACK. Ah, Contessa, I've been to Valenta—hardly a metropolis—but—

CONTESSA. But a larger population—a wider choice.

BLACK. Why, Anne, do I detect a note of reproach?

CONTESSA. I don't like promiscuity.

BLACK. I beg your pardon?

CONTESSA. I'm in no mood for your cheap humor.

BLACK. But you must be, or you wouldn't have made any comment about promiscuity.

CONTESSA. Nicki, shut up.

BLACK. Stop shouting at me. And stop pretending.

CONTESSA. I'm not pretending. After all, the Monsignor is in residence here.

BLACK. "In residence." Dear Contessa.
 [SHE *turns away*]
The shining white lady of virtue—look at her—radiant with a fine and holy light. In this state of grace have you told the Monsignor of your little plot?

CONTESSA.
 [*Turning to him*]
I don't want to talk to you, Nicki. You're drunk.

BLACK. Sober enough to know you're a fraud. I know why you're taking Paolo to Rome. You're not doing me a favor, you want him for yourself. Nerone is dead, but you'd like his son.

[*The* CONTESSA *tries to slap him.* HE *holds her hand*]
Dear Contessa—angel of the boudoir—mistress of the mattress—
[HE *releases her hand*]
You're a little old to be playing Aphrodite. Good night, Anne. Pleasant dreams.
[HE *staggers off the patio toward his room. The* CONTESSA *in shock and fright stares after him.* SHE *holds her cheeks—then shudders—then turns as* MEREDITH *enters*]

MEREDITH.
[*As* HE *enters* HE *starts to remove his cape*]
Contessa—
[SHE *rises to go*]
Please wait, Contessa. I would like to talk to you and Mr. Black.

CONTESSA. Mr. Black has gone to his room.

MEREDITH. Then I'll talk to you alone.

CONTESSA. Is it that urgent that you speak to me now?

MEREDITH. Yes—it is. I want to know your plans for Paolo Sanduzzi.

CONTESSA. Oh. I'm taking him to Rome—if his mother has no objections.

MEREDITH. She has.

CONTESSA. Perhaps she'll reconsider.

MEREDITH. Perhaps she will.
[SHE *doesn't answer*]
Is Mr. Black going to Rome with you?

CONTESSA.
*[Backing away]*
No. He is staying here—for a time.

MEREDITH. Then joining you later?

CONTESSA
*[Turning away]*
I don't know what his plans are.

MEREDITH. You do.
*[The* CONTESSA *doesn't answer]*
You do. Look at me, my dear Contessa.
*[*SHE *turns to him]*
You do know because his plans are yours. Terrible plans.
For you and for Mr. Black—and for the boy. Why did you
do it? Why do you want to hurt Paolo Sanduzzi?

CONTESSA. I don't want to hurt him—I want to help him.

MEREDITH. Do you?

CONTESSA. I—I don't know.

MEREDITH. Do you hate him because he is Nerone's son?

CONTESSA. No—no—that's why I love him. I hate him because he is Nina Sanduzzi's son.

MEREDITH.
*[After a pause]*
Tell me what you want to tell me, Contessa.

CONTESSA. Do you know all about Nerone?

MEREDITH. Almost all. I want to know if he was betrayed
—and by whom—and why—I know he came here the night
before his execution to ask—

CONTESSA. Yes—yes—to ask me to give Nina and his son refuge. First, Monsignore—know this about me—I've been married, widowed, and lusted too many times. I've known too many men—and not enough. I had too much pride to make myself available to the men in the village. But I wanted Nerone. That night when he came to see me and asked me for refuge for Nina and his son, I offered it provided he should come to me and spend the night with me. When he refused—I cursed him—I damned him.

MEREDITH. Finish all of it, Contessa.

CONTESSA. Later that night, I sent a message to Il Lupo and told him where he might find Nerone—I didn't know they were going to kill him. Tell me, Monsignore, will I be free now that I've told you?

MEREDITH. It's not that easy. Confession is a Sacrament in which pardon is given on an admission of guilt and a promise of repentance and reform—

CONTESSA. I do admit—I will admit.

MEREDITH. That's only halfway. The rest requires prayer —self-discipline—and the will to repair the harm already done.

CONTESSA. I'll try—I'll try—
> [*The* CONTESSA *suddenly breaks and cries hopelessly and help-lessly.* MEREDITH, *touched, rises to comfort her.* THE LIGHTS DIM *slowly as the scene ends*]

# Scene III

*The* LIGHTS COME UP *on the* CONTESSA'S *villa. It is late afternoon of the next day.*

A T  R I S E : BLACK *is sitting in a chair despondently waiting.* HE *rises as* PAOLO *enters on his way from the house.*

BLACK. Paolo.
> [PAOLO *stops.* HE *looks at* BLACK *and* BLACK *is aware instantly that something has gone wrong*]

Your face is sad. Tell me, Paolo, we have been friends.

PAOLO. You pay me to pose for a picture. I am not your friend.

BLACK. I am yours. I am glad you are going to Rome.

PAOLO.
> [*Turning to him*]

I am not going. The Contessa sent for me to tell me I am not going.

BLACK. Oh.

PAOLO. It is better I stay here in Gemello Minore with my mother.

BLACK. Did the Contessa also tell you that?

PAOLO. No. I think that myself.

BLACK. Soon I will be in Rome, Paolo. I'll send for you, if you'd like to come.

PAOLO. I would not like to.

BLACK. Believe me, Paolo. I think of you with friendship—or as I would of a young brother—whom I would like to see grow into a man—as good and strong a man as a brother I once had.
[PAOLO *shakes his head*]
I would see to it that you were educated and trained—

PAOLO. I will not grow to be a "femmenella."
[BLACK *drops his cigarette as* PAOLO *turns and exits.* BLACK *watches him go.* HE *lowers his head, then crosses to the wall and leans against it.* MEREDITH *appears carrying a folder.* BLACK *covers up his feelings as* HE *turns to* MEREDITH]

MEREDITH. Mr. Black—

BLACK. Mr. Prosecutor—how go your investigations?

MEREDITH. I've about finished the end of my work.

BLACK. You've been sparing with your observations—I'd enjoy hearing . . .

MEREDITH. Forgive me, Mr. Black.
[*The interruption serves to alert* BLACK]
The Contessa would be pleased if you would leave this villa as soon as possible.

BLACK. She might have had the politeness to tell me herself.

MEREDITH. I offered to do it for her. She is an unhappy woman who needs help.

BLACK. Which the Church is only too ready to give her. She's quite rich, isn't she?

MEREDITH. The Church would like to help you, too, Mr. Black—and you are poor, aren't you?

BLACK.
> [*His anger beginning to pile up*]

To hell with your help. I want nothing from you.

MEREDITH. I've brought something that might interest you.

BLACK. What is it? A tract from the Catholic Truth Society?

MEREDITH. Not quite. They are the personal papers of Giacomo Nerone. They were given to me last night by Nina Sanduzzi—would you care to look at them? He tells of his life—his sins—his ambitions—false and noble—his fears —his—

BLACK. Why do you show me this?

MEREDITH. Because it is a moving and spiritual record of a man who lost the Faith, as you have, and then came back to it. I felt it might help you.

BLACK.
> [*Sarcastically*]

You've been a marvelous help, Meredith.
> [*Then, hard and angry*]

You've helped to get me thrown out of this house. You've helped rob me of the last chance I had to finance an exhibition that might have re-established me—and you've helped to dirty the one decent thing I've ever tried to do.

MEREDITH. I don't understand that, Mr. Black—

BLACK. Then I'll be explicit. I'm talking about Paolo.
> [HE *sits on the table*]

The irony is, Meredith, that anytime in the last fifteen years

—you and all the rest of you—might have been right about my interest in Paolo. But—and listen to me, Meredith, and believe me—what I saw in him was everything that was lacking in my own nature. I wanted to educate him and make him what I could never be—a full man in body, intellect and spirit. If it meant denying every impulse to passion and every need I have for love and affection—I was prepared to do it. Paolo wouldn't believe me.

[HE *rises and pauses in front of* MEREDITH]

And you'd never believe it, would you?

MEREDITH. I might believe you, Mr. Black, but you could never do it—not without a singular grace from God. And how could you ask it, not believing?

[BLACK *stares at* MEREDITH *for a long moment*]

BLACK. Is that your only offer—the stale carrot of eternity?

[HE *turns*]

Please go, Monsignore. There is nothing you can do for me.

[MEREDITH *hesitates, embarrassed, then heads toward the house. Meanwhile,* BLACK *moves to the wall and stands on it with his back to the audience as he contemplates the height.* HE *is unaware of* MEREDITH, *or at least totally indifferent to him.* MEREDITH, *his back still to* BLACK, *hesitates, then stops.* HE *is aware of his lack of compassion but finds it difficult to articulate*]

MEREDITH. Mr. Black—truly I would like to—

[HE *pauses, searching for words.* HE *turns and becomes aware of* BLACK]

Mr. Black—

[*Then in horror*]

No!!

[*At that instant* BLACK *jumps from the wall as* THE LIGHTS DIM OUT]

# Scene IV

*When the* LIGHTS COME UP, *we are in the interior of* MEYER'S *house. It is night. His long sofa has been reconverted into a bed for* MEREDITH.

A T  R I S E : *The* CONTESSA *is seated in a chair.* SHE *is wearing a black coat over her dress.* SHE *has lost some of her pristine exactness in makeup and dress.* NINA *stands near the sofa.* FATHER ANSELMO *stands in the back of the room.* MEYER *is at the entrance, having just admitted* AURELIO.

MEYER.
[*To* AURELIO]
He has been asking for you.

AURELIO. Please tell me what happened—

MEYER. We can only guess. Nicholas Black obviously leaped from the wall at the Contessa's villa and rolled over four hundred feet down the hillside.
[AURELIO *nods and crosses to* MEREDITH]

MEREDITH.
[*Softly*]
Your Lordship—

AURELIO. I am here, my brother.
[AURELIO *takes* MEREDITH'S *hand.* MEREDITH *opens his eyes to make sure that* AURELIO *is present, and then* HE *nods*]

MEREDITH. You see—I had spoken to him—and had failed to give him the charity and understanding he deserved. I went down the hillside after him.

[HE *pauses for breath*]

I wanted to reach him and pray with him—it took me so long, so very long, to reach him. I said the Acts of Contrition, hoping that he would hear and join me—but he didn't. I gave him the last absolution. I failed him. I wanted to help—but I failed.

AURELIO. No one can judge failure but the Almighty.

MEREDITH. A man must judge himself first.

AURELIO. And then commit himself to mercy.

MEREDITH.
[*After a short pause*]
I'm dying, my Lord.

AURELIO. With dignity and among friends.
[MEREDITH *turns his head to look at* NINA]

MEREDITH. Where is your boy?

NINA. He is home. He is safe. He kissed my cheek and asked me to forgive him.

MEREDITH.
[*Softly*]
I'm glad of that.
[*A pause*]
You'll give Nicholas Black a Christian burial?

AURELIO. Who am I to deny him—

MEREDITH. You must write to Cardinal Marotta—tell him I have failed to complete my mission—tell him that my notes have proved Giacomo Nerone to be a man of great moral sanctity. It is for others to judge the merit of his Cause for Beatification.

AURELIO. I will tell his Eminence what you have said and I will see that your papers are sent to him.

MEREDITH. How are the oranges?

AURELIO. Ripening well.

MEREDITH. May I make a request?

AURELIO. Anything.

MEREDITH. I had asked to be buried in his Eminence's Church in Rome. I would rather be buried here. Explain to his Eminence that—that—Rome is very far—and here for the first time I have found myself as a priest and as a man.

AURELIO. Many of us have lived longer and done much less.

MEREDITH. I was afraid so long. Now, it's so very easy.
[*There is a pause and then* MEREDITH's *body quivers and his head rolls slackly into the pillow.* MEYER *places* MEREDITH's *hand over the dead priest's chest.* AURELIO *completes the gesture of finality by crossing* MEREDITH's *right hand over the left*]

AURELIO.
[*Softly*]
He is with God.
[*The* CONTESSA *has slipped from the chair onto her knees and bows her head.* NINA *gets to her knees. The bells begin to peal the Miserere as* AURELIO *and* ANSELMO *murmur the Latin responses*]

AURELIO. Requiem aeternam dona ei, Domine.

ANSELMO. Et lux perpetua luceat ei.

AURELIO. Requiescat in pace.

ANSELMO. Amen.

[*They both kneel.* AURELIO *throws himself across* MEREDITH'S *body*

[*As the bells peal,* THE CURTAIN FALLS SLOWLY]

*End of Play*